Introducti

The purpose of this book is to provide the student with a logical approach for learning to read music, develop keyboard technique, and thoroughly understand the basics of music theory. This book is especially written for the beginning mallet percussionist (who has yet to develop any bad habits on the keyboard), but can also be used by older students who would like to improve keyboard reading skills.

You will notice that music notation starts out quite large — actually "huge" would be a better word — and is generally printed on the lower half of the page. This is done intentionally to ease visual problems that are often associated with reading music on the bells with those "itty-bitty" keys. The note size decreases as you work your way through the book because, like it or not, you will eventually have to read "real" music at very small sizes!

It is my firm belief that solid learning comes through reinforcement. You will never see a new note or music theory concept introduced in this book without some repetition. Rather than just work your way through the book from start to finish, take a look at the Appendix, starting on page 44 in the back of the book. These written exercises and music reading studies will reinforce the fundamentals taught on each lesson.

The **MP3 / DATA CD** that is included provides a wealth of resources to supplement the book. You can play the accompaniments on any MP3 capable CD player - and access all of the files on a personal computer.

The **AUDIO ACCOMPANIMENT MP3's** are a great tool to make practice time fun. After you've spent the time to work up a tune, try playing along with the track, which includes a REAL percussion ensemble playing on REAL percussion instruments! In the process, you'll learn to use your ears to match the musical "phrasing" of the accompaniment parts.

There are a huge number of PDF's included on the CD that will help you become a great sightreader. The SPEED NOTE READING pdf has 120 lines to help you recognize notes on the treble and bass staves. For the student who might have had some piano training prior to beginning this method, the CD also includes each of the appendix lines transposed up an octave, into bass clef, and into "sharp" key signatures — so that he or she may read several versions of the same line in class with the other students.

As if this wasn't enough, the CD also includes the **"Speed Note Reading Tutor" video game**, a fun way to increase your sightreading skills by finding notes on a keyboard while racing the clock. And when you're ready to begin learning to play timpani, I've provided video lessons that you can watch that may help — especially if you do not have the benefit of regular private percussion lessons.

For band directors and percussion instructors, I've provided more suggestions and ideas on the "READ ME FIRST!" and "TEACHING THE BEGINNING MALLET PLAYER" files on the CD. Hopefully, some of these thoughts might spur new ideas of your own to keep the learning experience of your students fresh and exciting.

I've attempted to provide you with every possible resource so that you may accomplish one goal: to learn to play the keyboard percussion instruments, and HAVE FUN while doing it. As you work through the book, try to remember the golden rule: if you're not having fun, you're doing it wrong!

Good Luck!

Introducing a few of the most common mallet percussion instruments:

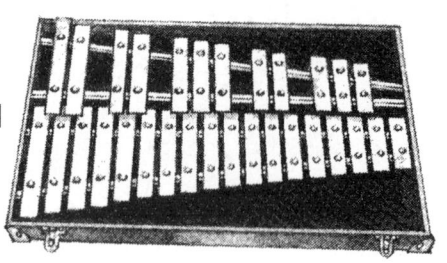

The **BELLS** (or **glockenspiel**) are made of steel and should be played with brass, hard plastic or rubber mallets.

The **XYLOPHONE** has rosewood or synthetic bars and should be played with "polyball", medium plastic, rubber or yarn mallets.

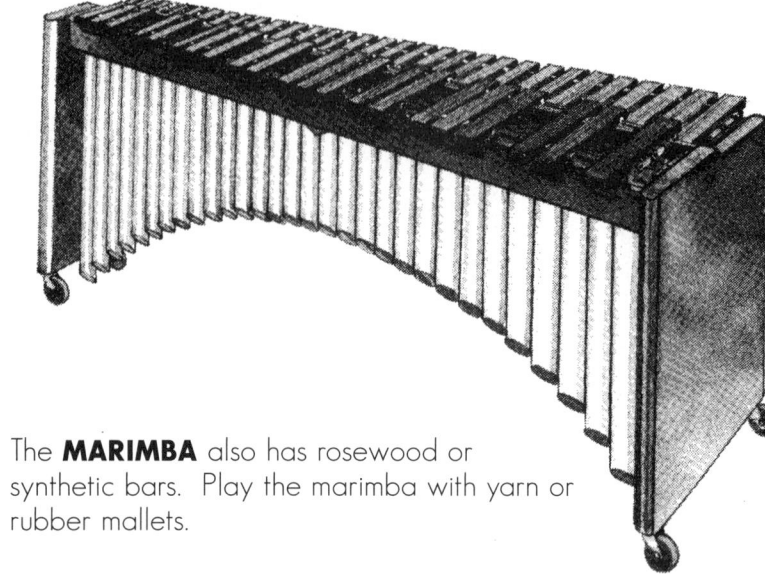

The **MARIMBA** also has rosewood or synthetic bars. Play the marimba with yarn or rubber mallets.

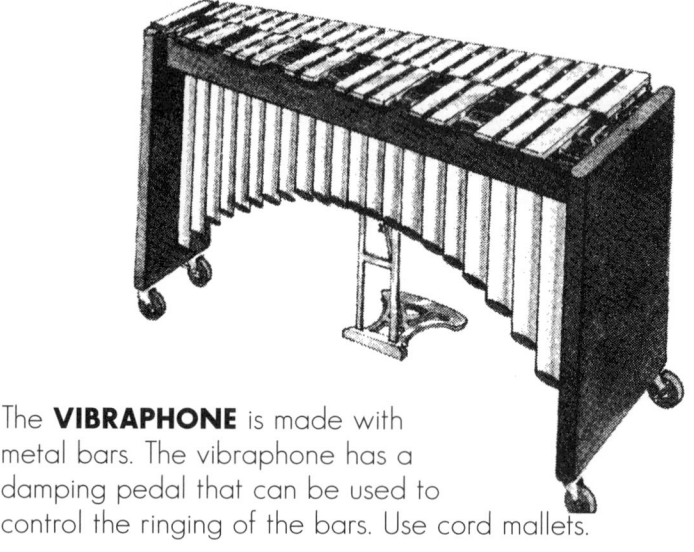

The **VIBRAPHONE** is made with metal bars. The vibraphone has a damping pedal that can be used to control the ringing of the bars. Use cord mallets.

Playing position

Adjust the height of your bell set until it's about 4 inches below your waist.

Position the music stand as close to the keyboard as possible. The bottom of the stand should almost touch the raised bars. If you're playing on a marimba or vibraphone, the music stand and music should be centered in front of the keys that the piece requires.

Stand about 6-8 inches away from your instrument so that you can easily reach the center of each bar. Stand up straight with your feet slightly apart and weight distributed evenly on both feet.

As you eventually move up and down the keyboard, you'll be required to "sway back and forth" — that is, move your upper body to the right and left while keeping your feet in place.

The grip and stroke

1. Place the mallet diagonally across your open hand from the middle joint of the index finger across the "heel" of your hand.

2. Grasp the mallet between the fleshy part of the thumb and the middle joint of the index finger about 4 inches from the end of the shaft. The contact point between the thumb and the index finger is called the "fulcrum."

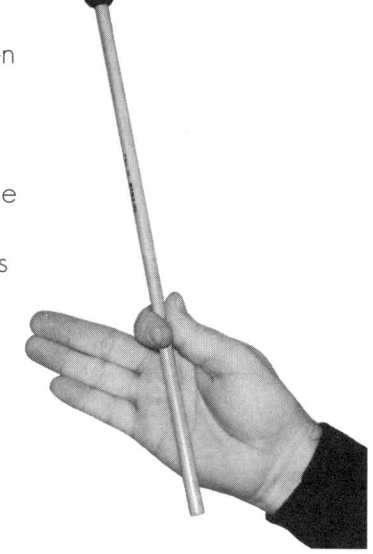

3. Wrap the remaining three fingers loosely around the mallet.

4. Stand behind the instrument with your arms relaxed by your side. Raise the mallets to the instrument by bending at the elbow, keeping the shoulders and upper arms relaxed.

5. Learning a relaxed stroke is simple. Without the mallets in your hands, wave "bye-bye." Notice that the hand is very relaxed and the arm is not used to produce the motion. This is the relaxed wrist motion you'll use to produce the stroke.

6. Place the mallet in your hand and try to produce the same relaxed wrist-only motion by playing in the air on an imaginary keyboard. The goal is to produce the stroke with the wrists and back fingers as relaxed as possible — and to keep the motion isolated to the wrist (don't pump the forearm up and down).

Beginning Exercise

Using the diagram, find the notes F and C on your keyboard. Play the following sticking patterns in the middle of each bar. Think of "pulling the sound out of the bar."

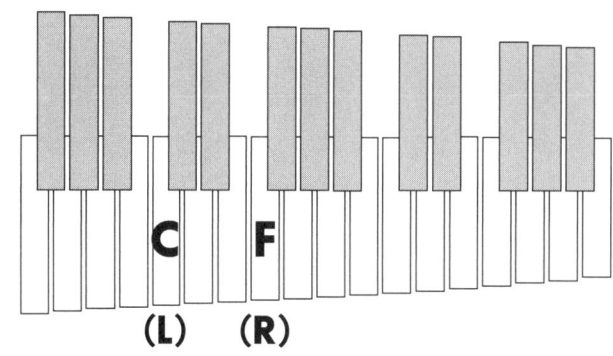

1. **R R R R   R R R R   L L L L   L L L L**

2. **R R R R   L L L L   R R R R   L L L L**

3. **R R L L   R R L L   R R L L   R R L L**

4. **R L R L   R L R L   R L R L   R L R L**

* TEACHERS: You can use these sticking patterns as a quick daily warm-up by applying various notes and scales

Step 1: Learning the Basics

Music Theory

Before we start using the keyboard, there are some very important aspects of the musical language that you need to learn.

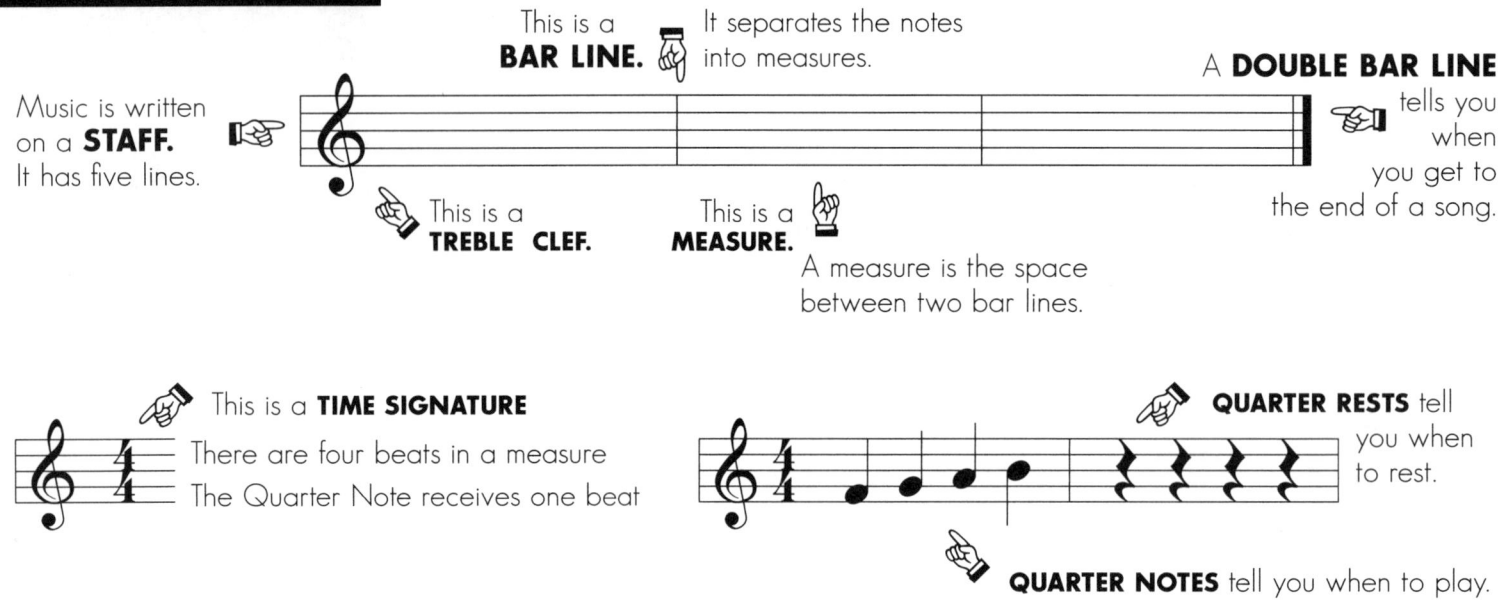

Music is written on a **STAFF**. It has five lines.

This is a **BAR LINE**. It separates the notes into measures.

This is a **TREBLE CLEF**.

This is a **MEASURE**. A measure is the space between two bar lines.

A **DOUBLE BAR LINE** tells you when you get to the end of a song.

This is a **TIME SIGNATURE**
There are four beats in a measure
The Quarter Note receives one beat

QUARTER RESTS tell you when to rest.

QUARTER NOTES tell you when to play.

Pencil Games
It's time to practice what you've just learned, so get a pencil and learn to write your OWN music!

① Learn to draw the TREBLE CLEF.

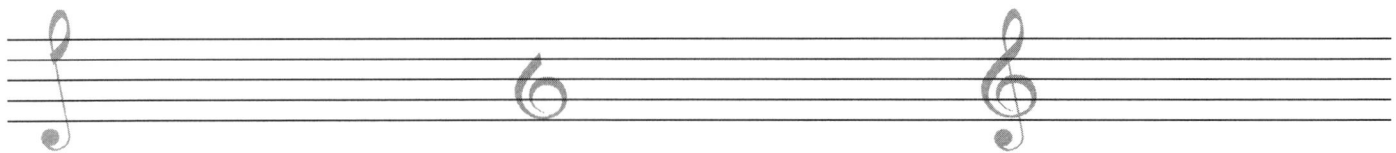

Trace the first loop & tail, then try 3 of your own.

Now trace the bottom loop. Draw 3 that look as good!

Use both steps to trace the Treble Clef. Practice on two or three of your own.

② Draw some Quarter Notes

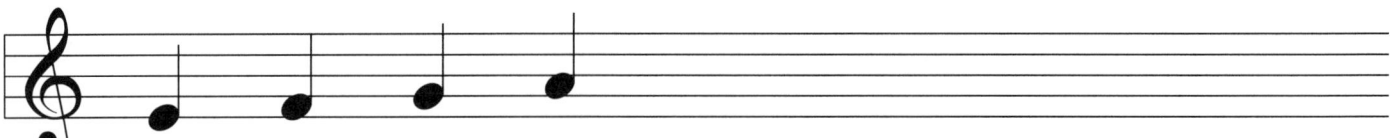

On quarter notes <u>below</u> the middle line, the stem attaches to the RIGHT side of the note head and goes UP. Practice on a few quarter notes BELOW the middle line.

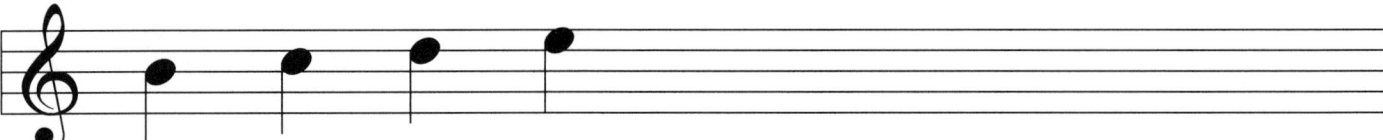

Now draw a few quarter notes <u>on or above</u> the middle line. The stem on these notes should attach to the LEFT side of the note head and go DOWN.

Step 2: Learning the Musical Alphabet – introducing the keyboard!

 Music Theory

The <u>raised</u> keys are called **ACCIDENTALS** and are arranged in groups of two or three. You can use these accidentals as landmarks for locating the naturals.

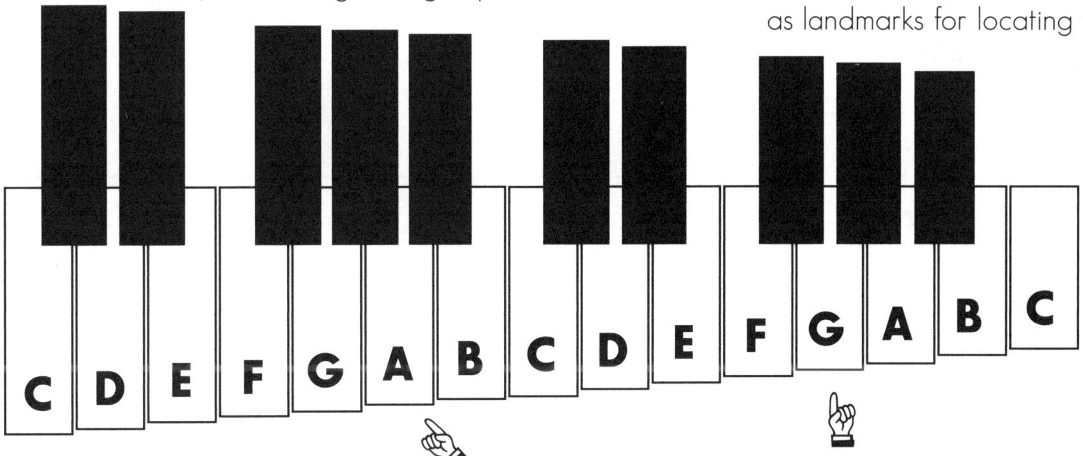

The <u>lower</u> keys are called **NATURALS**.   The **MUSICAL ALPHABET** uses the letters A to G

Pencil Games
Fill in the blanks to show your knowledge of the musical alphabet. You must be able to go forwards (UP the alphabet) <u>and</u> backwards (DOWN the alphabet).

FORWARDS:
① A __ __ __ __ __ __ G
② C __ __ __ __ __ __ B

BACKWARDS:
③ G __ __ __ __ __ __ A
④ D __ __ __ E

Step 3: Using the Musical Alphabet on the Treble Staff

The **LINES** of the treble staff spell: **E**lvis' **G**uitar **B**roke **D**own **F**riday

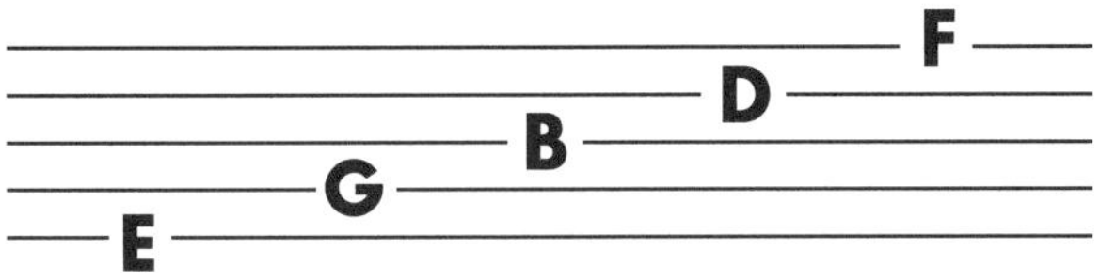

The **SPACES** of the treble staff spell: **"F-A-C-E"**

Pencil Games
Fill in the note names for the quarter notes in the following blanks.

* The Appendix on page 44 has more music theory exercises that you can use to check for mastery of this lesson. And for extra practice on naming notes on the treble staff, refer to the SPEED NOTE READING document on the CD.

5

Learning to Count Quarters in 4/4 Time.

Each quarter note and rest receives ONE BEAT in a "Quarter" Time Signature. Write in the counts under the quarter notes in the following exercises, then clap the rhythm while you count out loud.

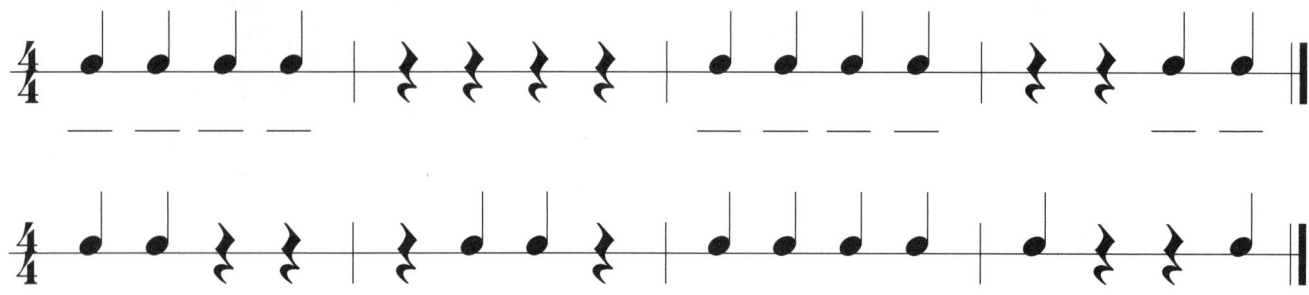

 A **Flat Sign** lowers the pitch of a note one **half step**. A HALF STEP is the distance from any key to the very next key — above or below.

 OUR FIRST NOTE: **B♭** (B flat) is one <u>half</u> <u>step</u> lower than the note B.

 The note **B♭** is the top note in the group of THREE accidentals.

1

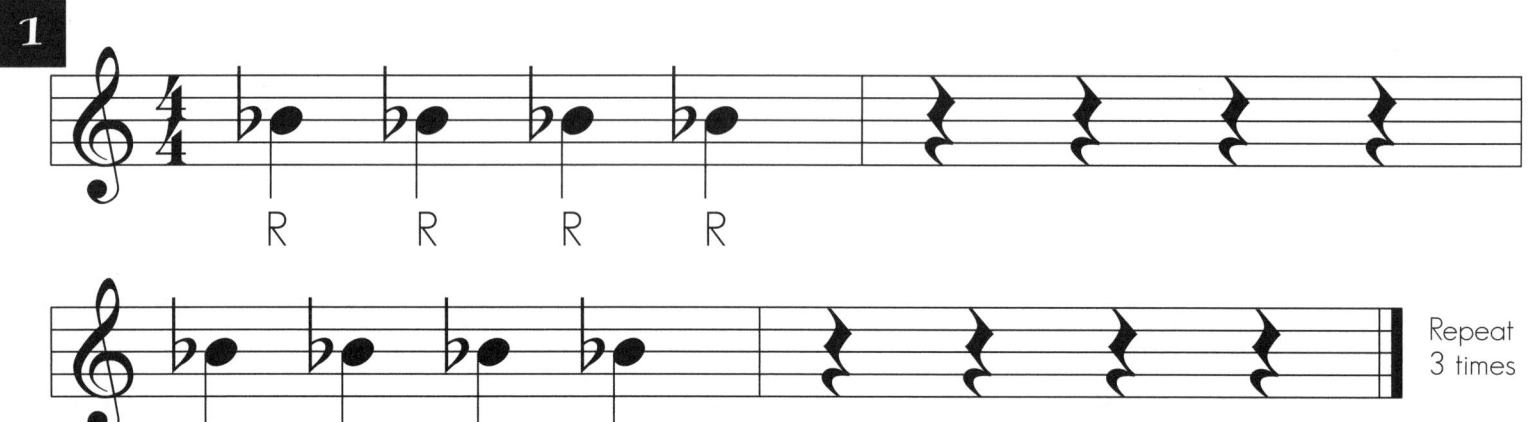

Repeat 3 times

2 Try to play this line without looking down at all! Play the entire line with the right hand, then a 2nd time with the left.

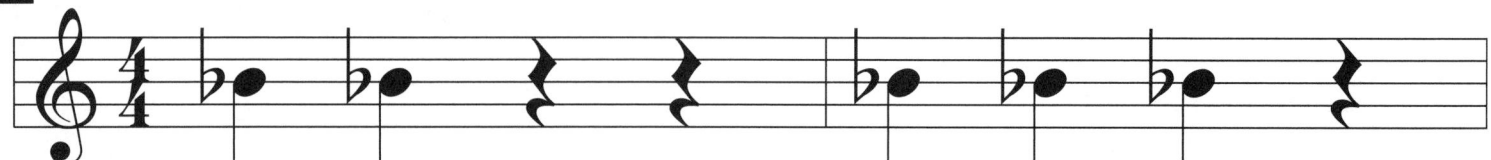

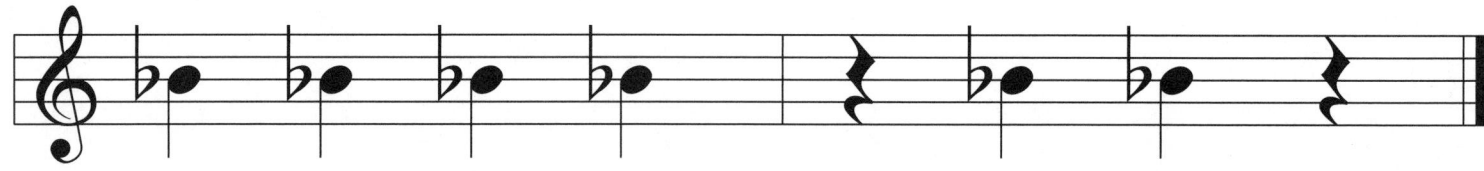

6

Pencil Games

Write the name of each note from the treble staff in the blank provided. The **Appendix**, located on page 45, also provides several **"Speed Tests"** for finding notes on the treble staff.

* I highly recommend completing 4-5 lines of the SPEED NOTE READING document on the CD each day. Getting faster at recognizing the notes on the treble staff with these lines is the best way I've found to teach music reading skills!

New Note

The NEW NOTE: **A♭** (A flat) is one half step lower than the note A.

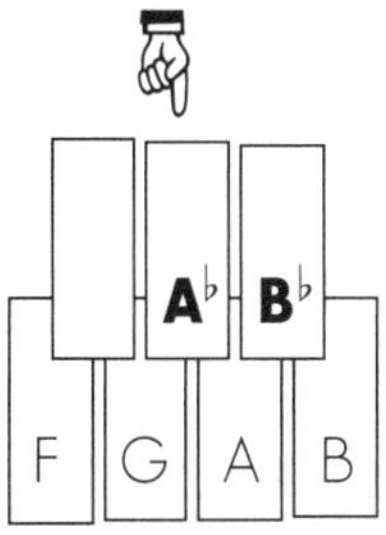

The note **A♭** is the MIDDLE note in the group of three accidentals.

3 Whenever a flat appears in a measure, it remains in effect for the ENTIRE measure.

4 Position the music stand as close to the keyboard as possible. Lower the stand until it almost touches the accidentals.

The Half Note and Half Rest

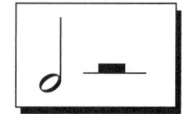

Music Theory

A **Half Note** or **Half Rest** receives TWO counts when beating time to the quarter. Here is an example:

Add the bar lines in the following example, then write in the counting under the notes. When you finish, count the rhythm out loud to a metronome.

Time yourself to see who is the fastest in your class! Add 2 seconds for each wrong answer.

Speed Test

* You're now ready to play LEVEL ONE of the **Speed Note Reading Tutor** video game included on the CD. In this fun computer game, you'll race the clock to name the notes on the treble staff. Try competing against with a friend to find out who is fastest!

Music Reading

Can you "see" your keyboard while looking at this page? This ability is called the **peripheral vision**. Use your peripheral vision to find the keys while you keep your EYES on the MUSIC!

5

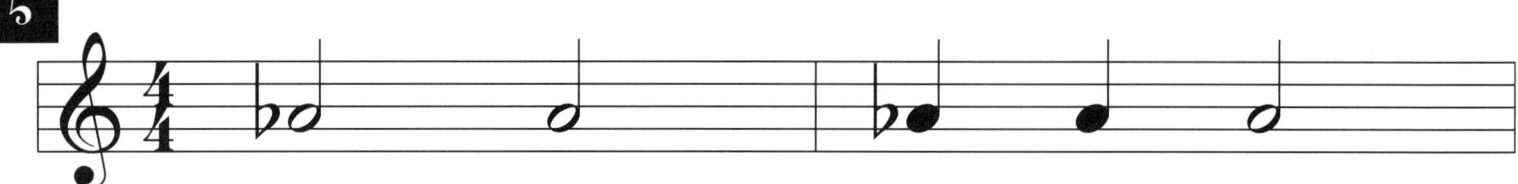

Pencil Games

Use the musical alphabet to find the note on the keyboard. Remember that the note **F** is the first natural below the group of three accidentals.

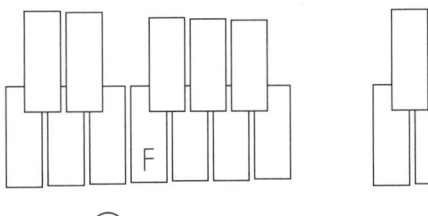
① **A**

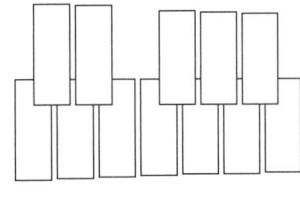
② **B**

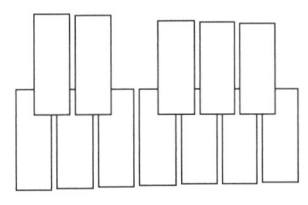
③ **E**

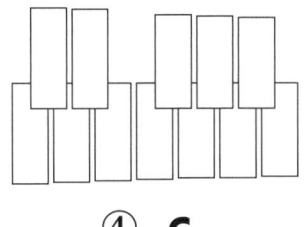
④ **C**

* For more "note finder" practice, play LEVEL TWO on the **Speed Note Reading Tutor** video game!

The new note **G♭** is one WHOLE STEP below the note **A♭**

New Note

A **Whole Step** is equal to two half steps. Skip a key . . . natural or accidental.

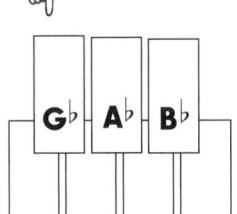

6 Without looking at the keyboard, play through each exercise with your fingers (piano style). Since you can actually FEEL the keys, you don't have to look down AT ALL!

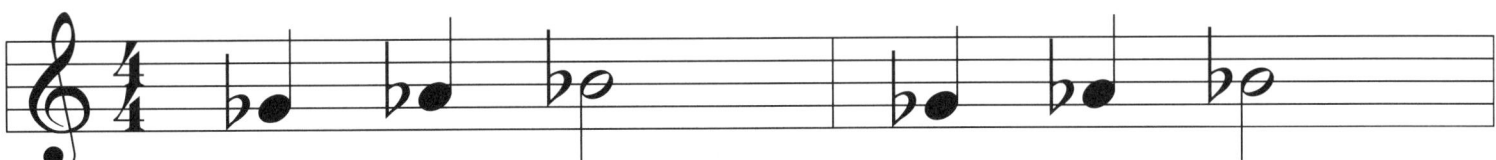

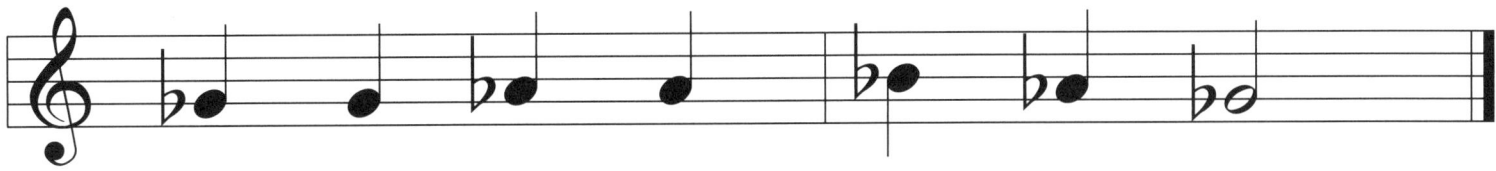

7 "Finger through" each line and say the note names out loud to a metronome BEFORE you attempt to play it.

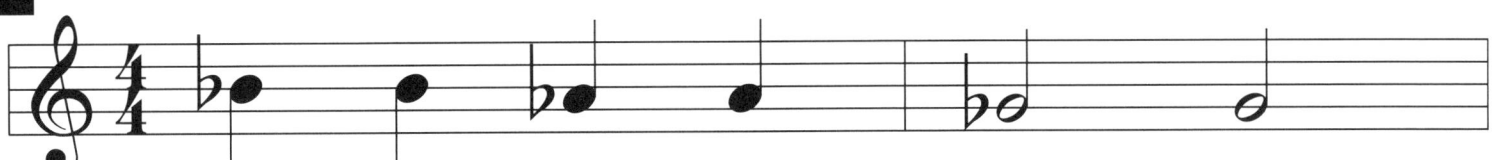

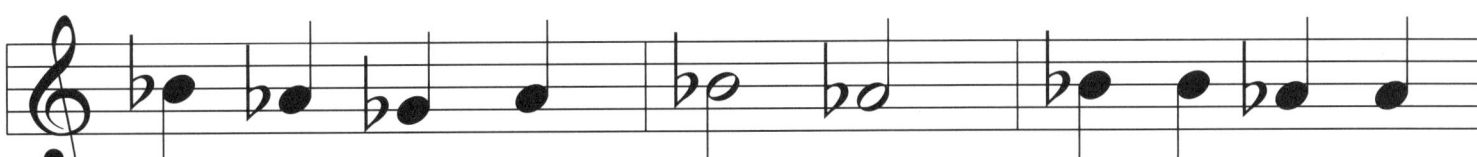

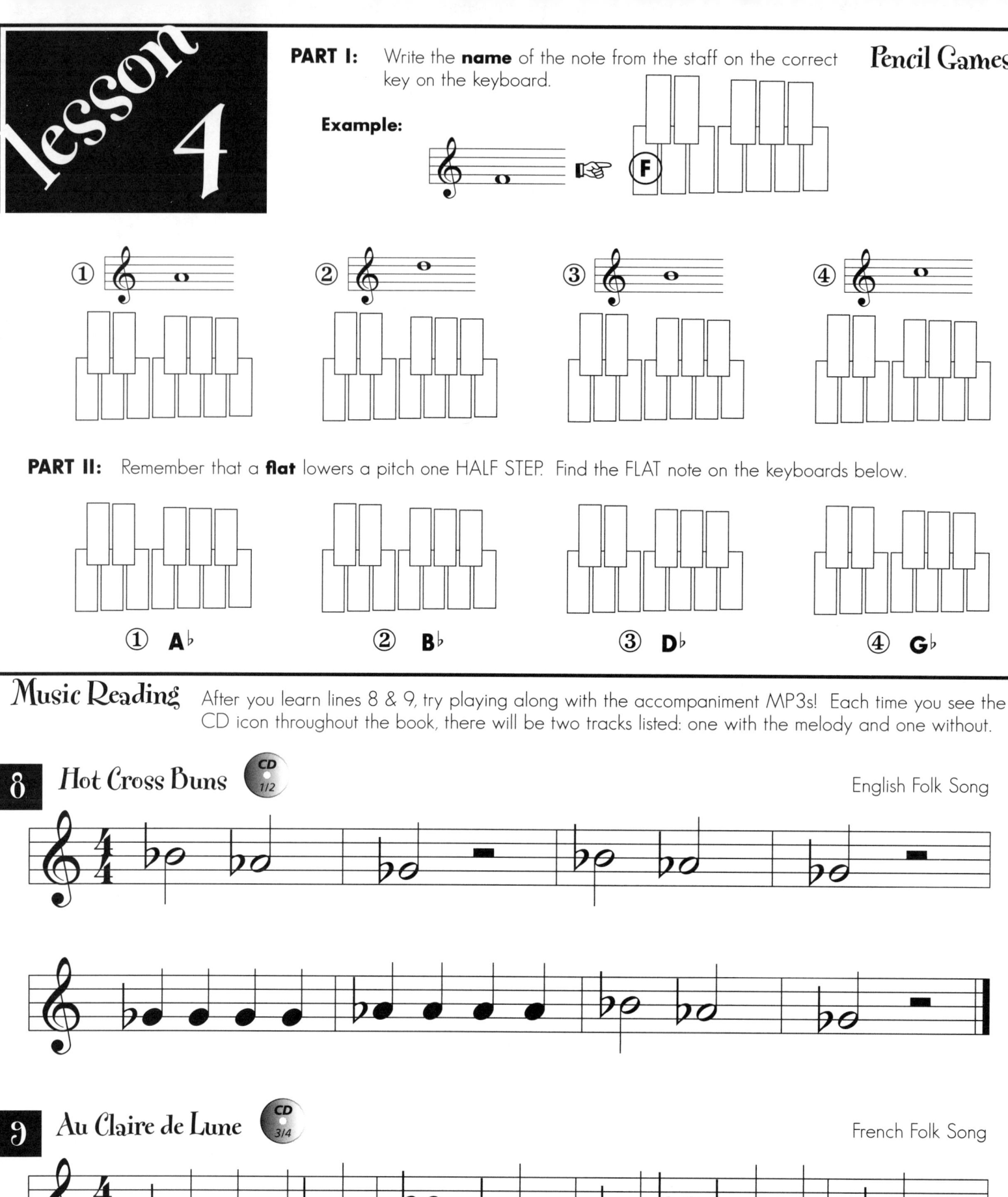

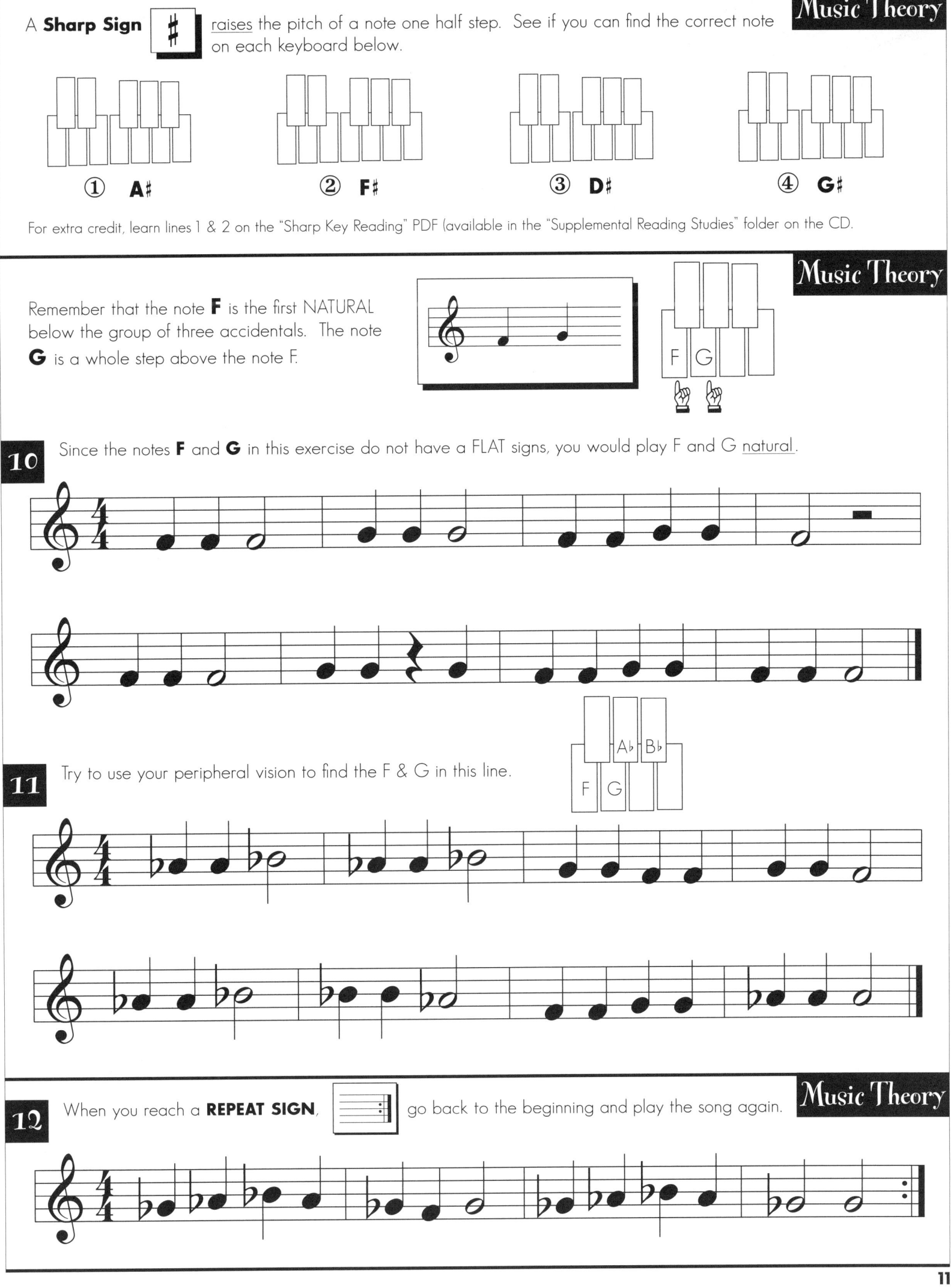

Lesson 5

Tetrachords — Music Theory

A **tetrachord** is a series of 4 notes having the pattern of whole step, whole step, half step. Tetrachords are the building blocks of the major scales.

Using the starting notes below, build the 4 notes of the tetrachord.

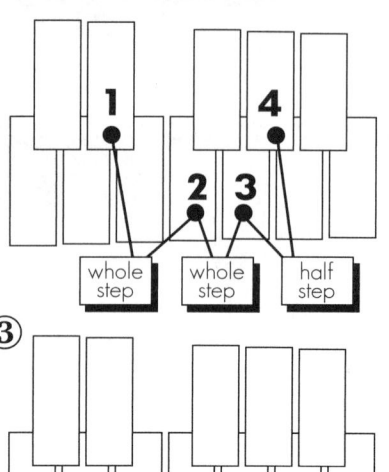
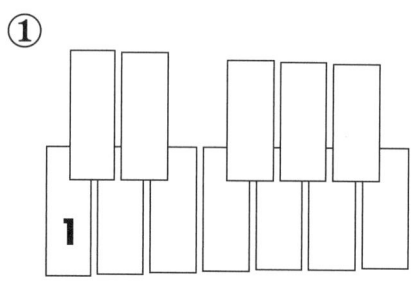
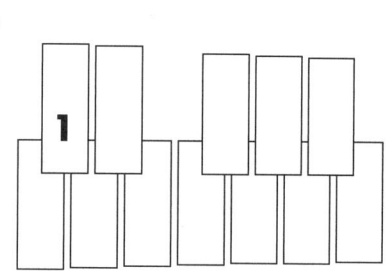
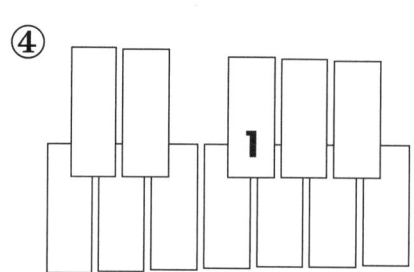
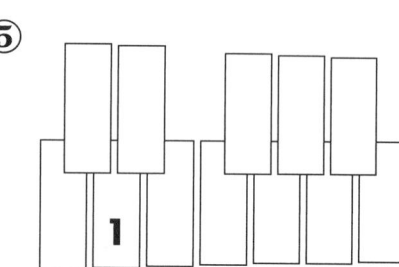

C Tetrachord

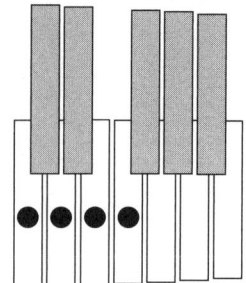

The first tetrachord to memorize starts on C. Play this short exercise everyday as part of your warmup. As we learn more tetrachords, we will link them together to build the major scales.

When practicing tetrachord exercises:
- Use full wrist strokes • Practice with a metronome to ensure a steady tempo • Strike each note in the center of the bar

Music Reading

Try to ALTERNATE your sticking in this exercise. Remember to "finger through" and say the note names <u>out</u> <u>loud</u> BEFORE you attempt to "sightread."

13 CD 5/6

12

G Tetrachord

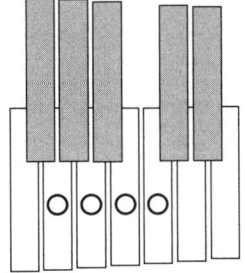

Now, memorize the G tetrachord and add this exercise to your daily warmup.

Once you've memorized the C and G tetrachords, you can begin building the MAJOR SCALES. Memorize a new tetrachord each week and build new scales following the examples on page 92.

New Note

The new note **E♭** is the top note in the group of TWO accidentals.

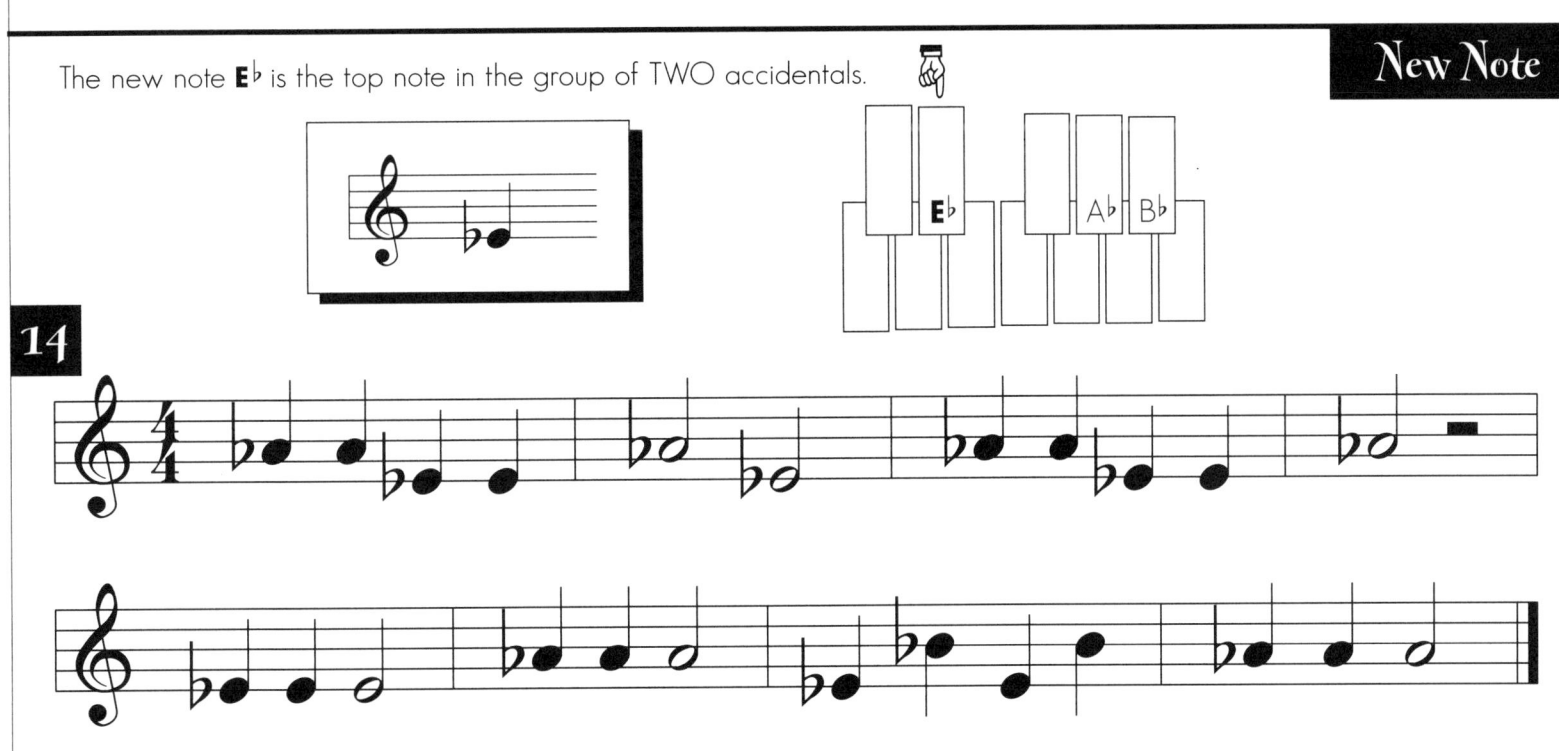

14

15 Mary Had a Little Lamb – Duet

Traditional

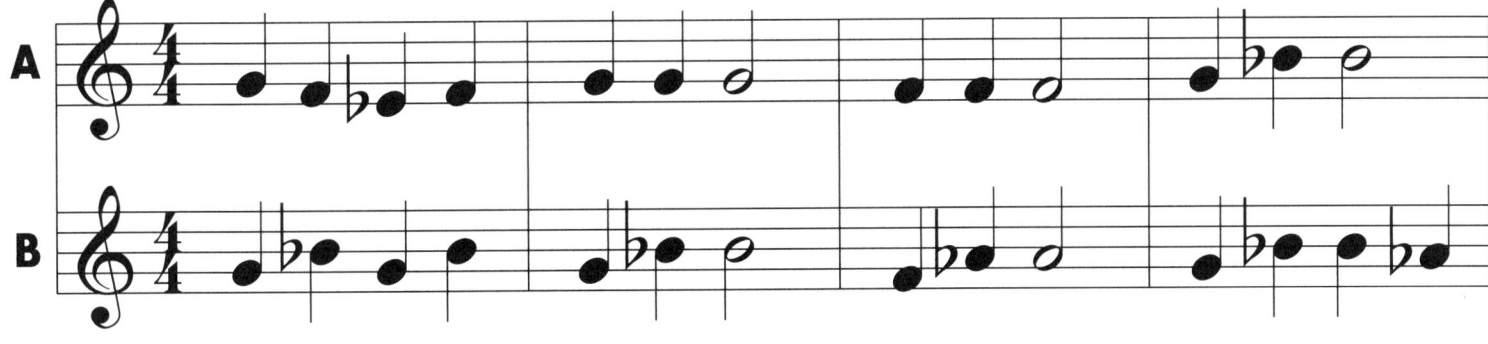

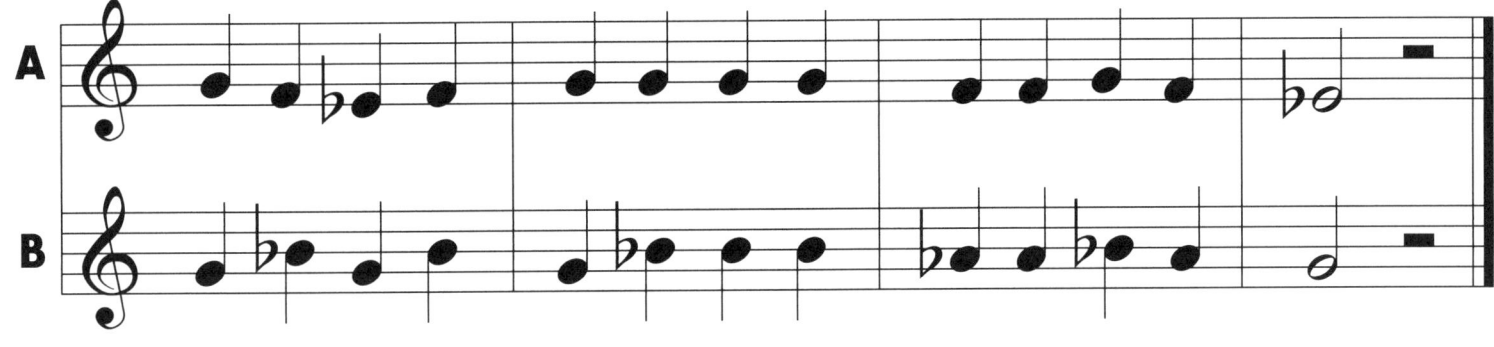

13

Ledger Lines

Ledger Lines are used to extend the range of the staff (much like rungs on a ladder). Notice that you will use the musical alphabet to "walk" up or down this musical ladder.

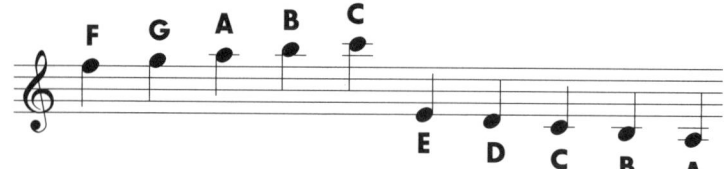

Fill in the blanks to spell the correct note names

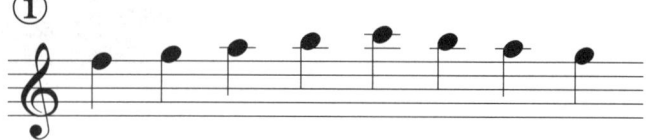

The new note **D** is the first note BELOW the staff, the new note **C** uses a **ledger line**.

New Note

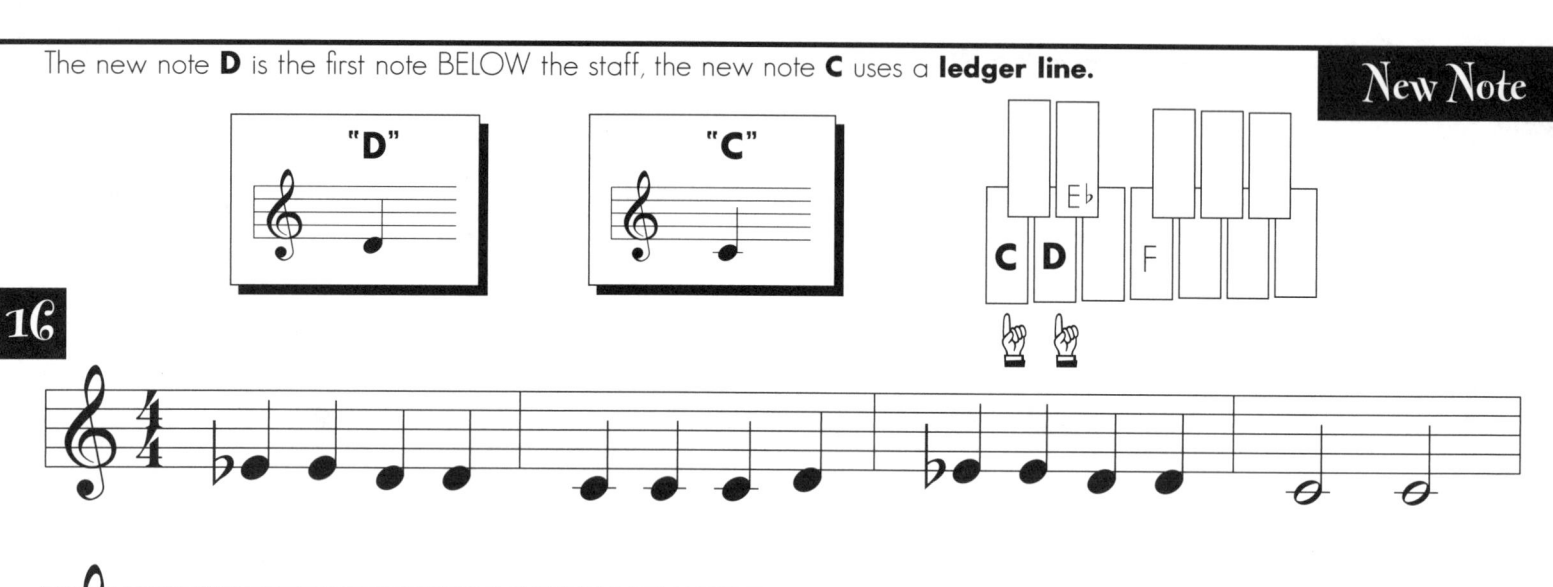

16

The Whole Note
A Whole Note or Whole Rest receives 4 beats in quarter time.

Music Theory

Draw in the bar lines, then write the counting under the notes. Count this line out loud to a metronome when you finish.

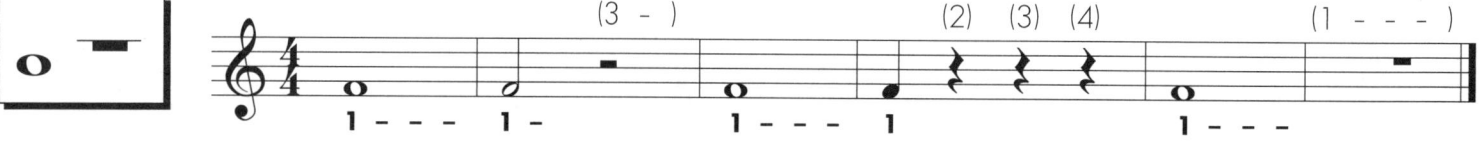

Eighth Notes

There are two 8th's in each quarter note. Any 8th note that falls between the down beats is counted "and" or "te."

Example:

Write the counting under the notes in the following exercises, then clap the rhythm while you count out loud to a metronome.

①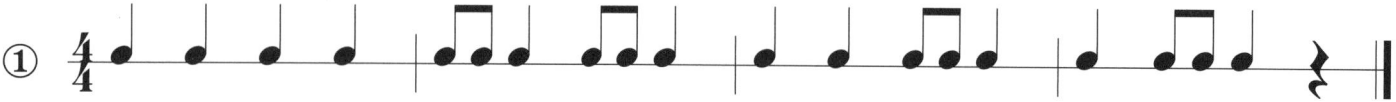

②

③

Music Reading

The following familiar song is written with 8th notes. See if you can guess the name **without** playing it on the keyboard first!

19

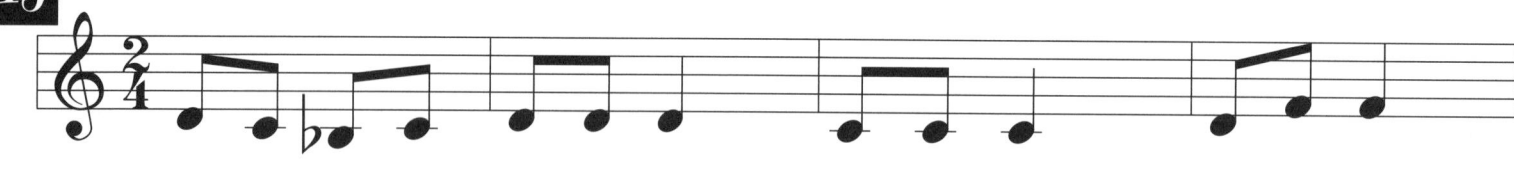

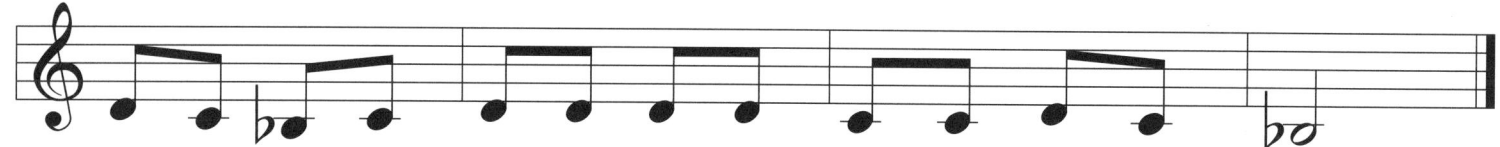

20 Baa, Baa, Black Sheep   *Traditional*

16

Music Theory

Key Signatures

Accidentals placed at the beginning of a piece of music change those notes throughout the entire piece.

Notice that this key signature would make ALL **B's** and **E's FLAT.**

Since these notes are also B & E, the key signature would make them B♭ and E♭.

Write the names of the accidentals that appear in the **key signature**, then CIRCLE the quarter notes that are affected.

① ___

② ___ , ___ , & ___

③ ___

Music Reading

You may wish to draw a flat by the notes affected by the key signature in the following lines.

21 Jolly Old St. Nicholas American Christmas Carol

22 The Counting Song Traditional

17

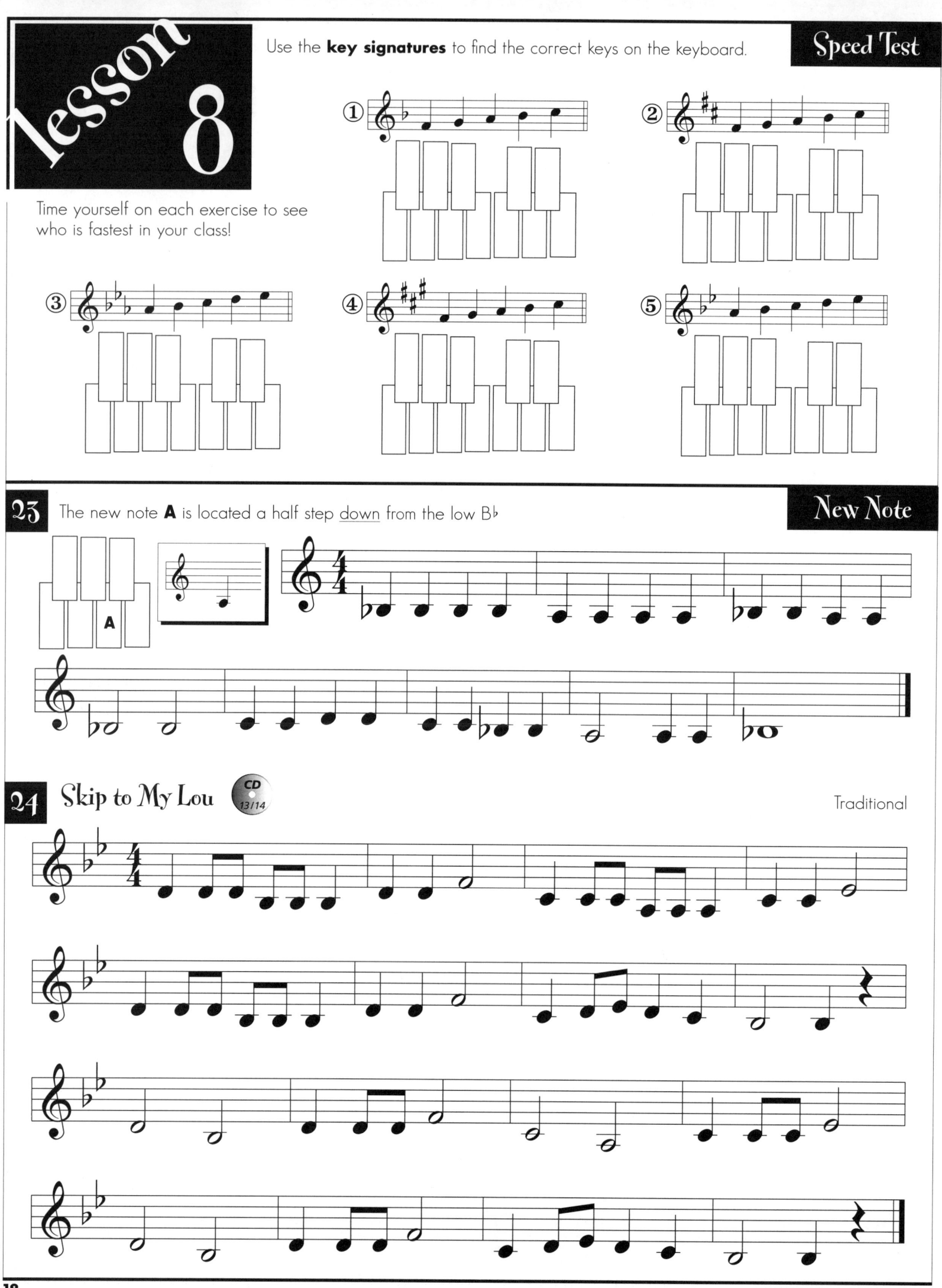

Dotted Half Notes — Music Theory

A **Dot** placed after a note increases a note's value BY HALF of the original value. Since a half note is equal to TWO counts in quarter time, a **dotted half note** would get THREE counts.

Example: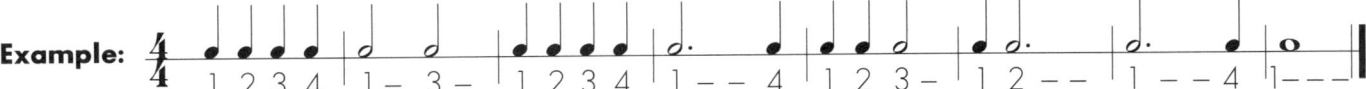

In the following example, draw in the bar lines and write the counts under the notes.

25 — New Note

This song uses the new notes **A♭** and **D♭**. You really don't have to repeat it 99 times!

Repeat Ad Nauseum

Music Theory

Pick-Up Notes begin **before** the first measure and are borrowed from the last measure.

26 Oh, Susannah

Stephen Foster

CD 15/16

19

Lesson 9

Note Value Test — Music Theory

Add the note values together to find the total number of beats in quarter time.

Music Reading

The second part of this duet uses **"double-stops"** — two notes played at the same time.

27 Shortnin' Bread   Traditional

Check the key signature to find out whether this note is **A♭** or **A natural**.

28 Rakes of Mallow   English "Gigue"

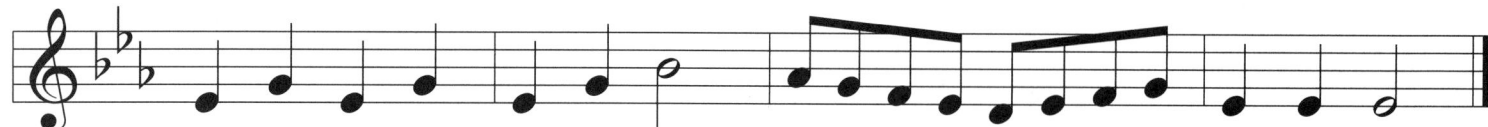

29 And _ingo Was His Name American Folk Song

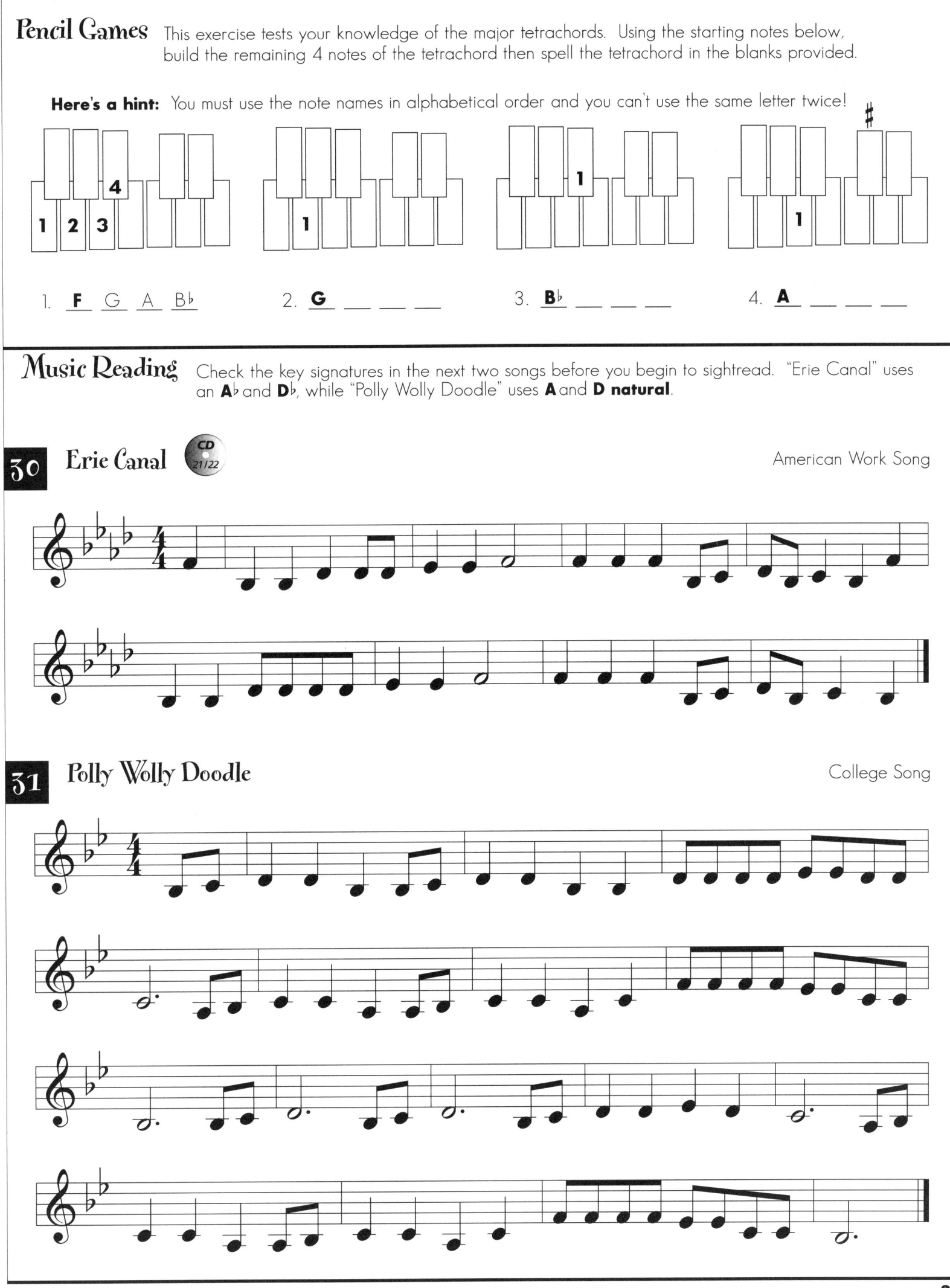

Lesson 10

Music Theory

Ties

A **tie** connects two notes of the same pitch. The 2nd note is added in value to the 1st.

Example:

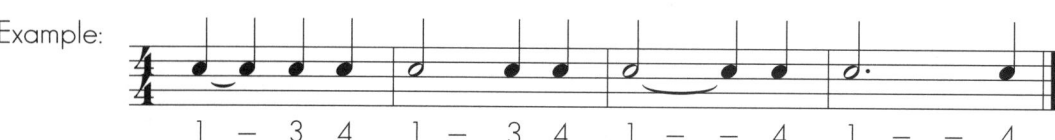

1 – 3 4 1 – 3 4 1 – – 4 1 – – 4

Write the counts under the notes, then clap the rhythm while you count out loud to a metronome.

Music Theory

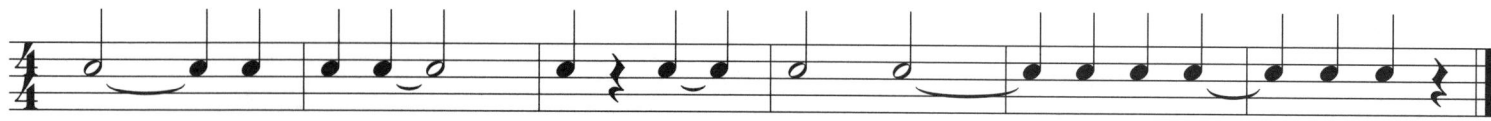

First and Second Endings

In this example, you would play the first ending (the measures under the first bracket), then repeat. The second time through, skip the first ending and play the second ending.

32

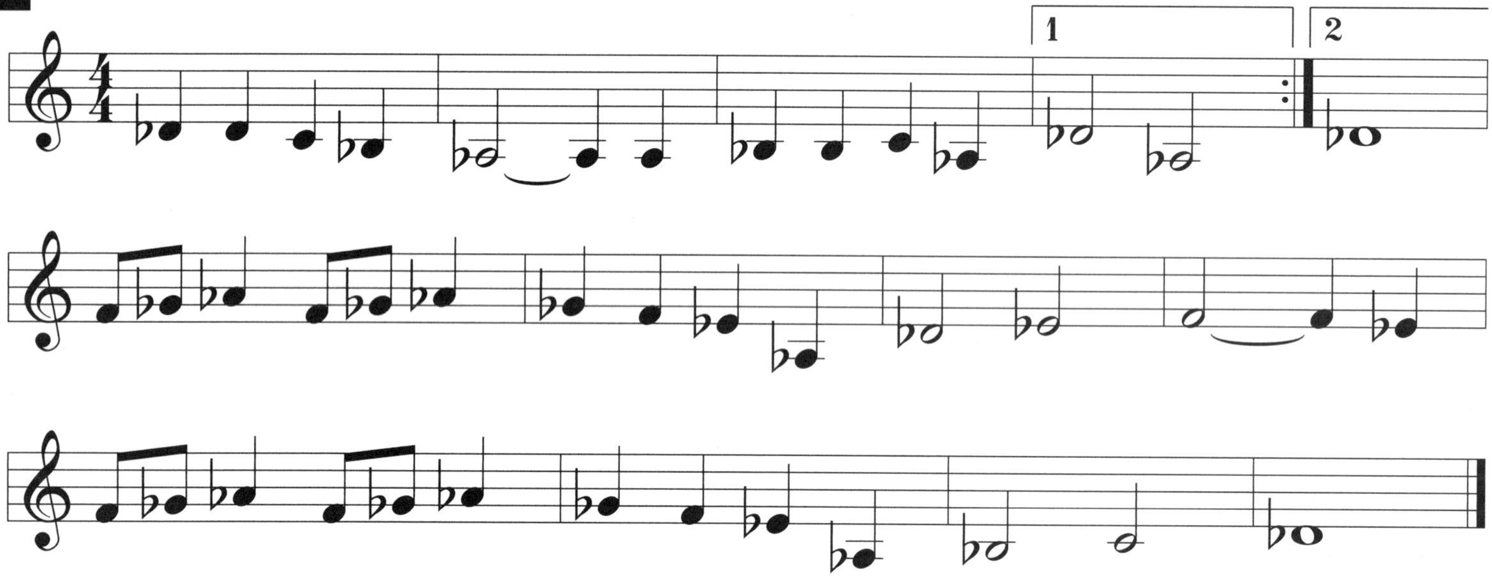

33 Old MacDonald CD 23/24

Traditional

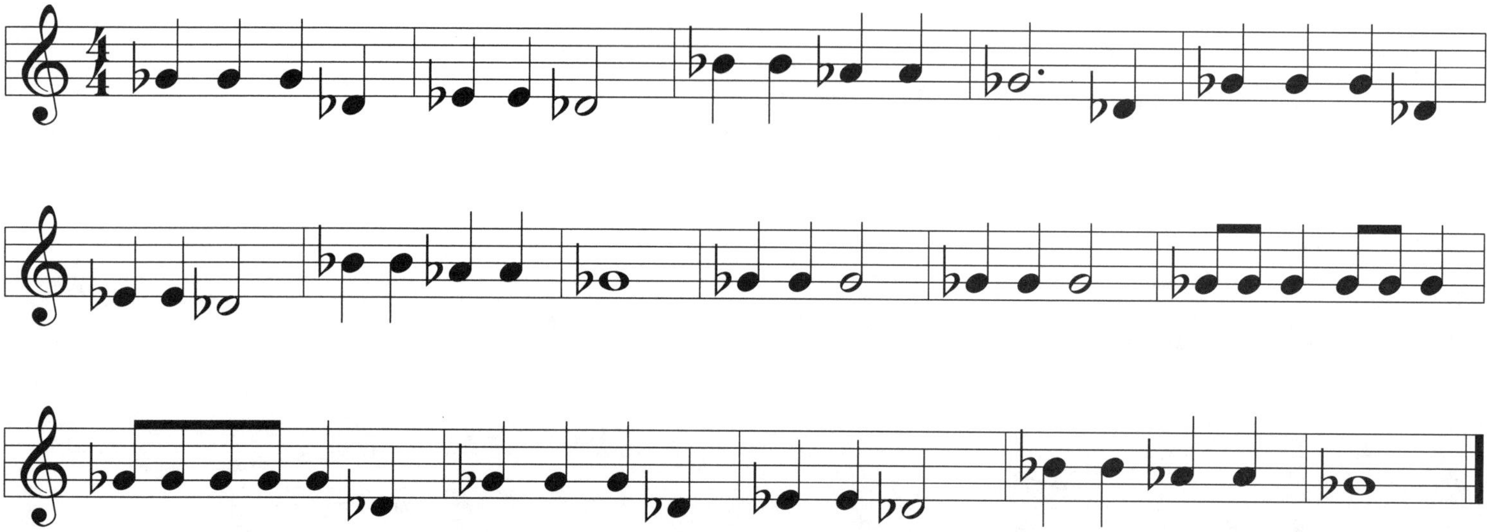

Pencil Games

Part I: Using whole notes, draw these notes ON the staff (don't forget the accidentals where necessary). You may only use a line or a space <u>once</u>.

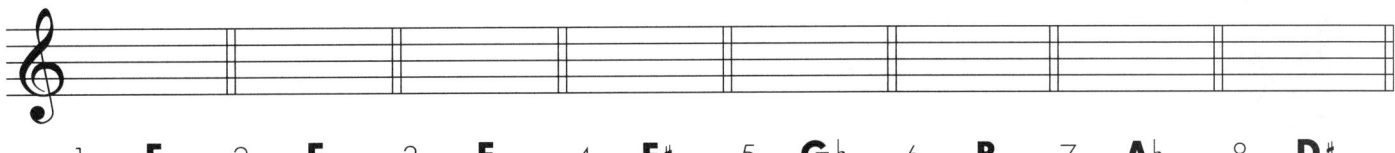

1. **F** 2. **E** 3. **E** 4. **F♯** 5. **G♭** 6. **B** 7. **A♭** 8. **D♯**

Part II: Using ledger lines, draw these notes ABOVE the staff (you may not use the top line of the staff).

1. **G** 2. **B** 3. **D** 4. **A♯** 5. **C** 6. **E♭** 7. **B♭** 8. **F♯**

Music Reading

This version of the melody in Beethoven's Ninth Symphony includes **double-stops**. You may wish to work up each part separately before you put both hands together.

 **34** Ode to Joy
Ludwig Van Beethoven

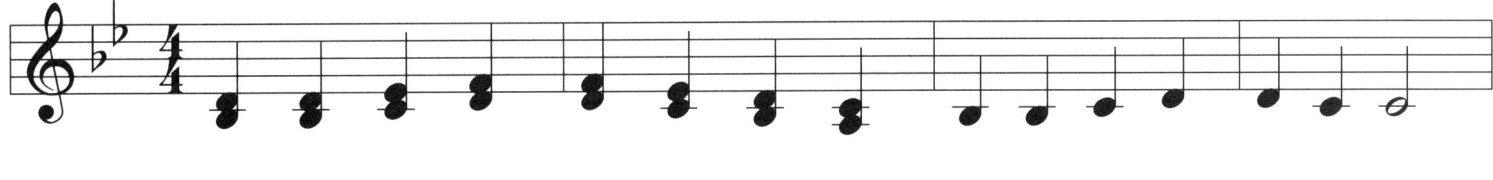

The **ROLLS** (notes with slashes) included in the next song are explained on page 90 in the back of the book. Work up this etude <u>without</u> the rolls first, then add them to put on the "finishing touch" on the song.

 **35** When the Saints Go Marchin' In
Traditional

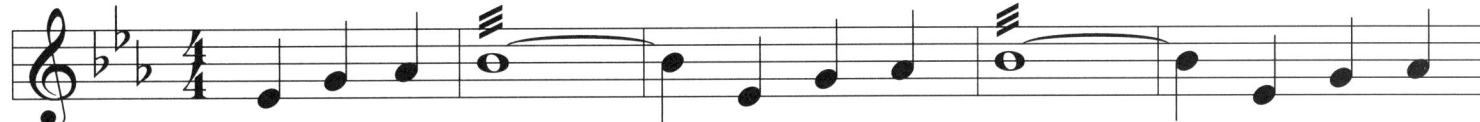

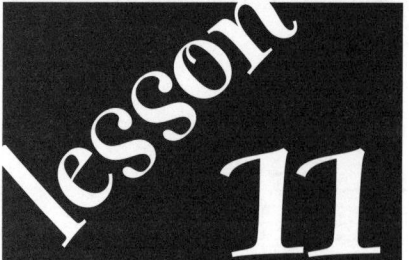

Music Math — Music Theory

Part I: Write the number of beats that each pair of notes would receive.

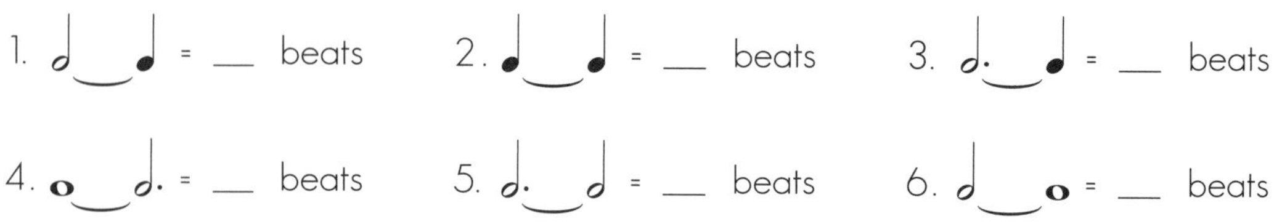

1.  = __ beats
2.  = __ beats
3.  = __ beats
4. 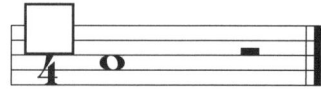 = __ beats
5.  = __ beats
6.  = __ beats

Part II: Count the number of beats in each measure and fill in the missing number in each time signature.

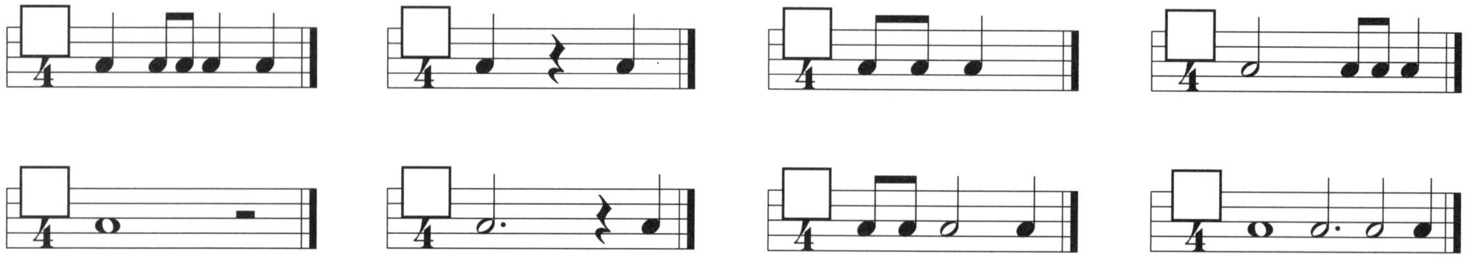

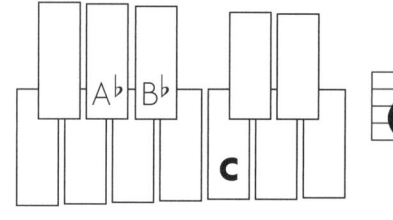

36 The new note "C" is located on the third space of the treble staff. — Music Theory

When a **FERMATA**  is placed over a note, roll that note until your director signals you to stop.

37 American Patrol — Meacham

Music Theory

A **Natural Sign** ♮ is sometimes used to <u>cancel</u> a sharp or a flat in the key signature. It remains in effect throughout the entire measure.

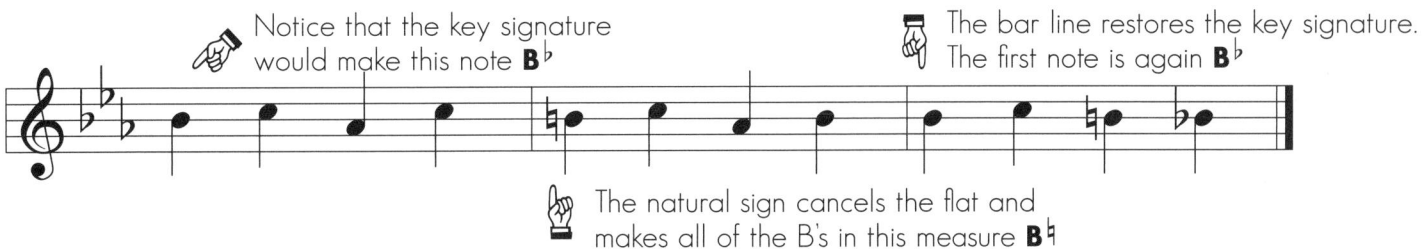

Exercise: Write the note names in the blanks provided. Draw a NATURAL SIGN on all note names that are not flat.

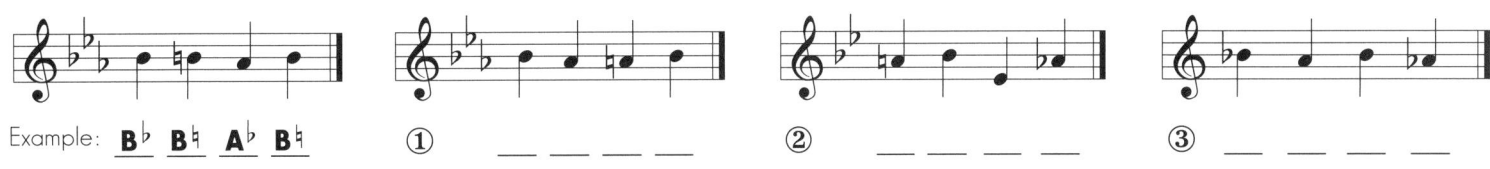

Example: B♭ B♮ A♭ B♮

① ___ ___ ___ ___

② ___ ___ ___ ___

③ ___ ___ ___ ___

Music Reading

This song uses a NATURAL to <u>cancel</u> the key signature. The A♮ returns to A♭ in the 2nd line.

38 Surprise Symphony

Joseph Haydn

New Note

39 Since this song only uses four notes, try to play it without looking at the keyboard AT ALL! Try to <u>alternate</u> your sticking as much as possible.

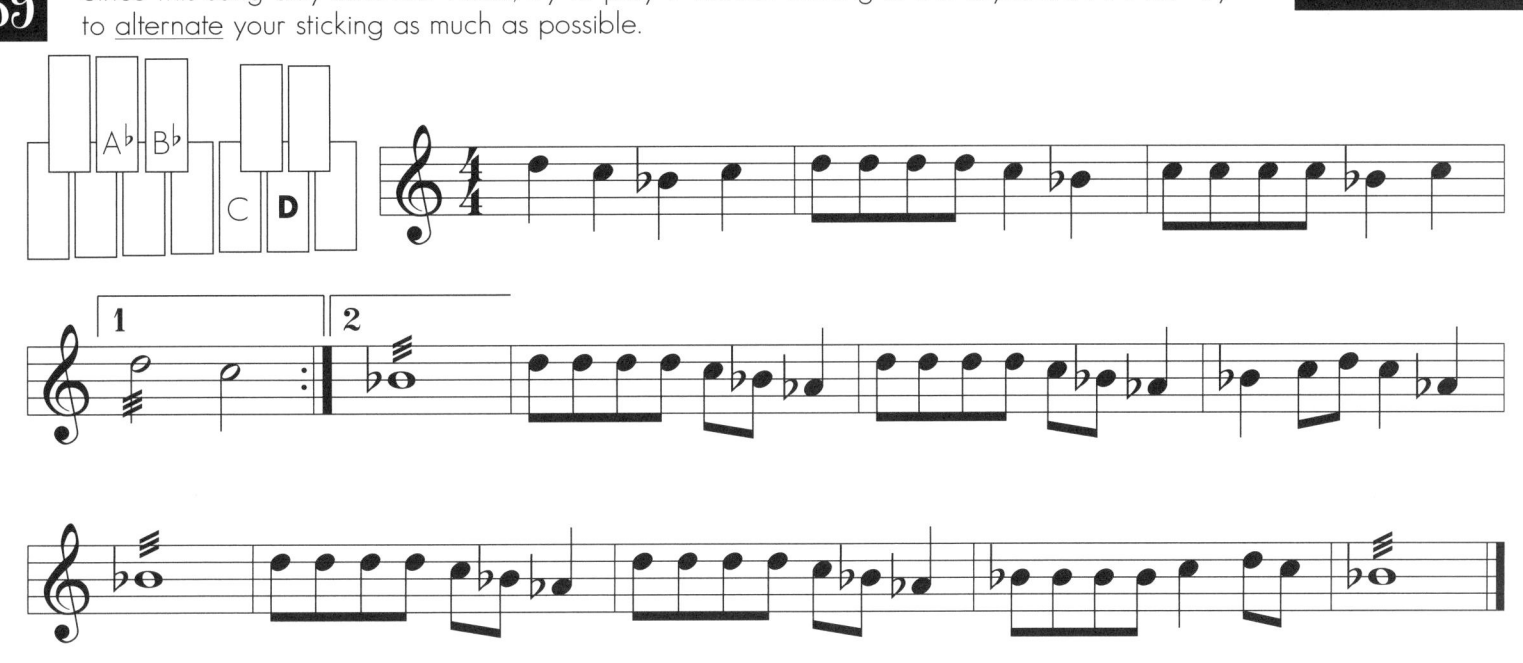

The Bass Clef

Music Theory

The **Bass Clef** is used for many percussion instruments including timpani. All percussionists should be able to read music written in the bass clef.

The lines of the bass clef spell:

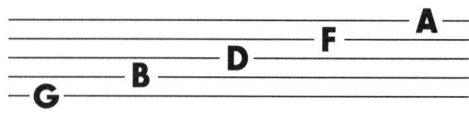

Good – Boys – Do – Fine – Always

The spaces spell:

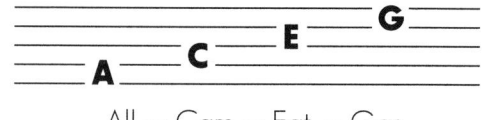

All – Cars – Eat – Gas

Exercise: See if you can guess the words that these notes spell (using the **Bass Clef**).

① ___   ② ___   ③ ___   ④ ___

Part II: Using quarter notes, spell these words on the staff (can you remember which direction the stems go?)

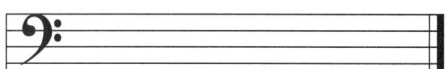 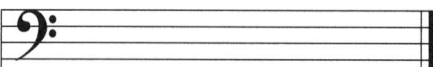 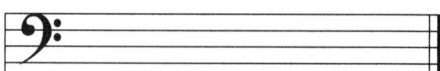

① C – A – B   ② B – A – G   ③ F – E – E – D

40   The new note **E♭** is on the top space of the treble staff.   **New Note**

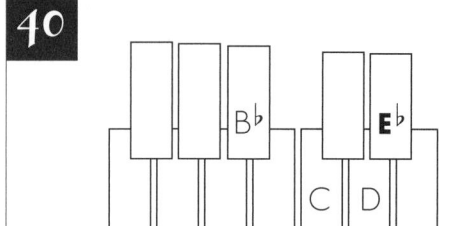 

41 Kookaburra Round

Australian Folk Song

See if you can always look ahead to the NEXT note while playing the rolls in this exercise. How fast can you play this line without missing a single note? (NO FAIR MEMORIZING!)

Speed Test

26

Major Scales and Arpeggios

After you've learned to put two tetrachords together to build a major scale, it's important to learn to play it using a common scale rhythm pattern: one quarter followed by 8th notes. Practice the C Major Scale by repeating this scale pattern several times:

An ARPEGGIO is tones of a chord broken into individual notes. The C major arpeggio is the first, third and fifth notes of the major scale (plus the octave):

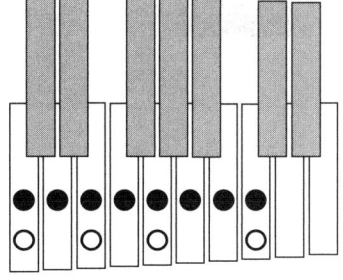

The Major Scales and Arpeggios are listed on page 94-95 in the back of the book. A good percussionist should know all 12 by memory!

Music Reading

The Bach "Serenade" could have been written with first and second endings. Can you find where the first ending, repeat sign and second ending signs would have been placed?

42 Yankee Doodle (CD 31/32) — American Folk Song

43 Serenade (CD 33/34) — J.S. Bach

Lesson 13

Music Theory

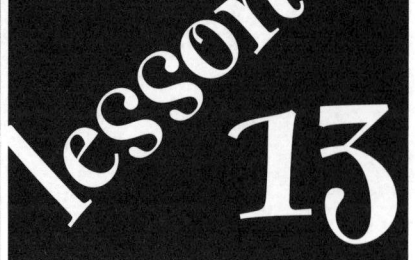

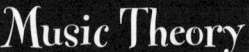

Dotted Quarter Notes

Remember that a dot placed behind a note or rest increases its value by half of the original value. Since there are two 8th notes in a quarter, a **dotted quarter note** would be equal to three 8th notes.

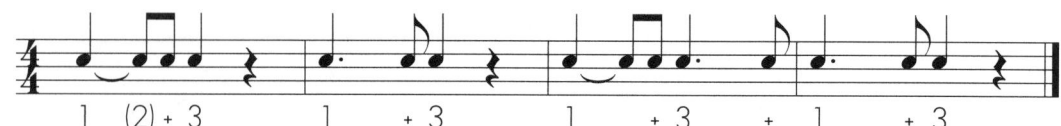

Write the counts under the notes, then clap the rhythm while you count out loud to a metronome.

Music Reading

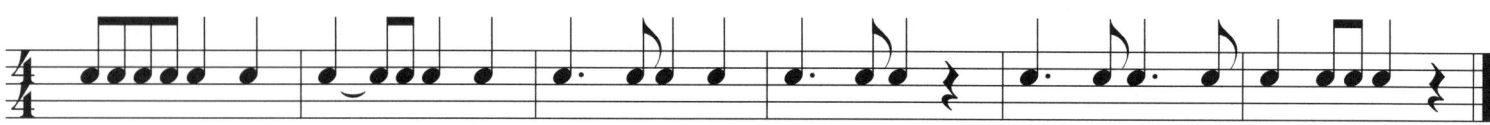

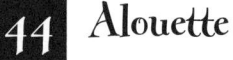

Are you still "fingering through" each song, saying the note names BEFORE you sightread? Remember to always keep your eyes on the music, not on the keyboard!

44 Alouette

French-Canadian Folk Song

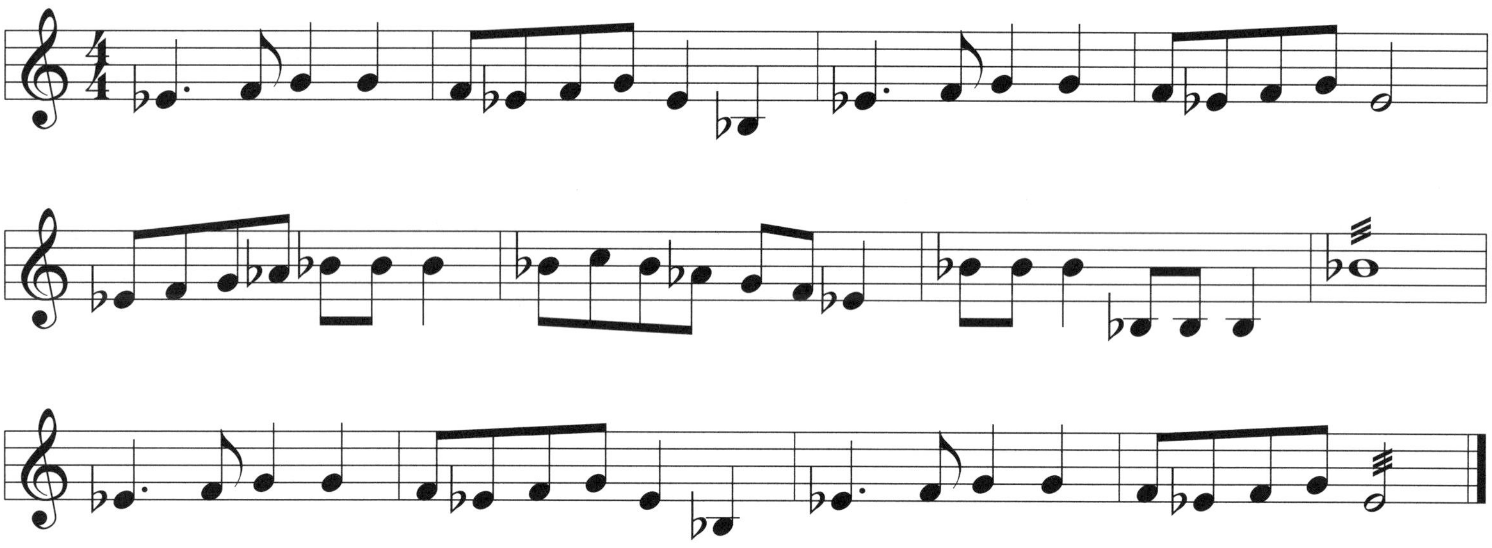

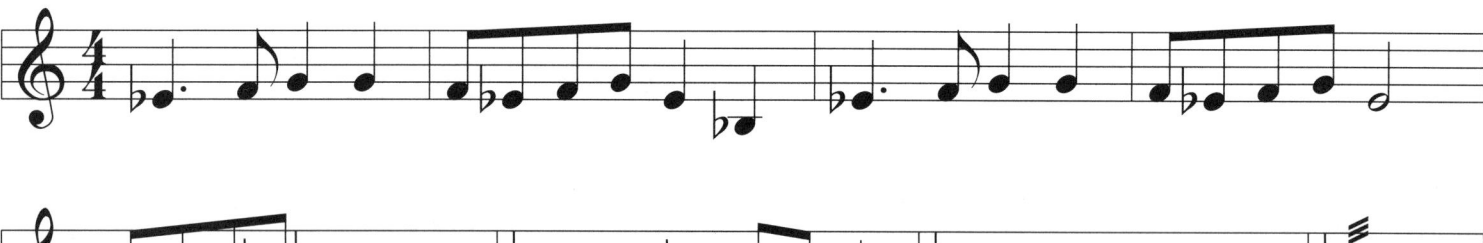

45

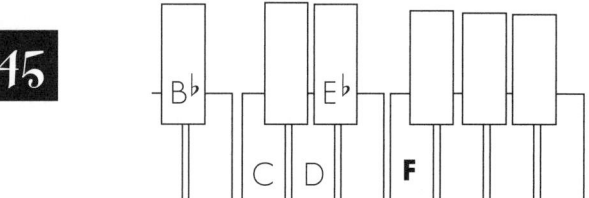

New Note

The new note "F" is located on the top line of the treble staff.

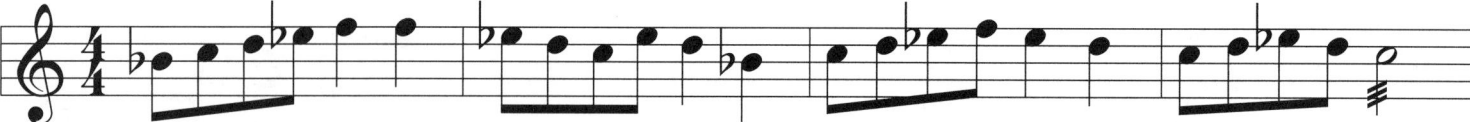

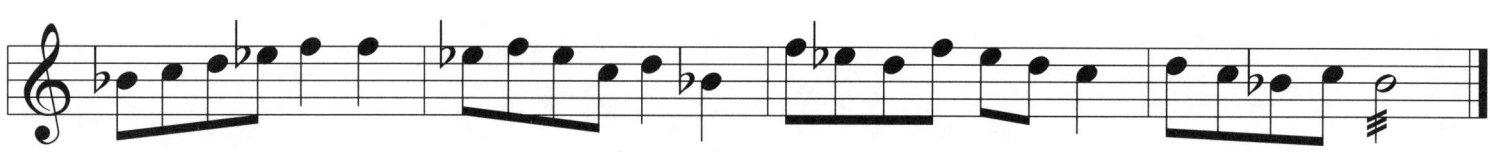

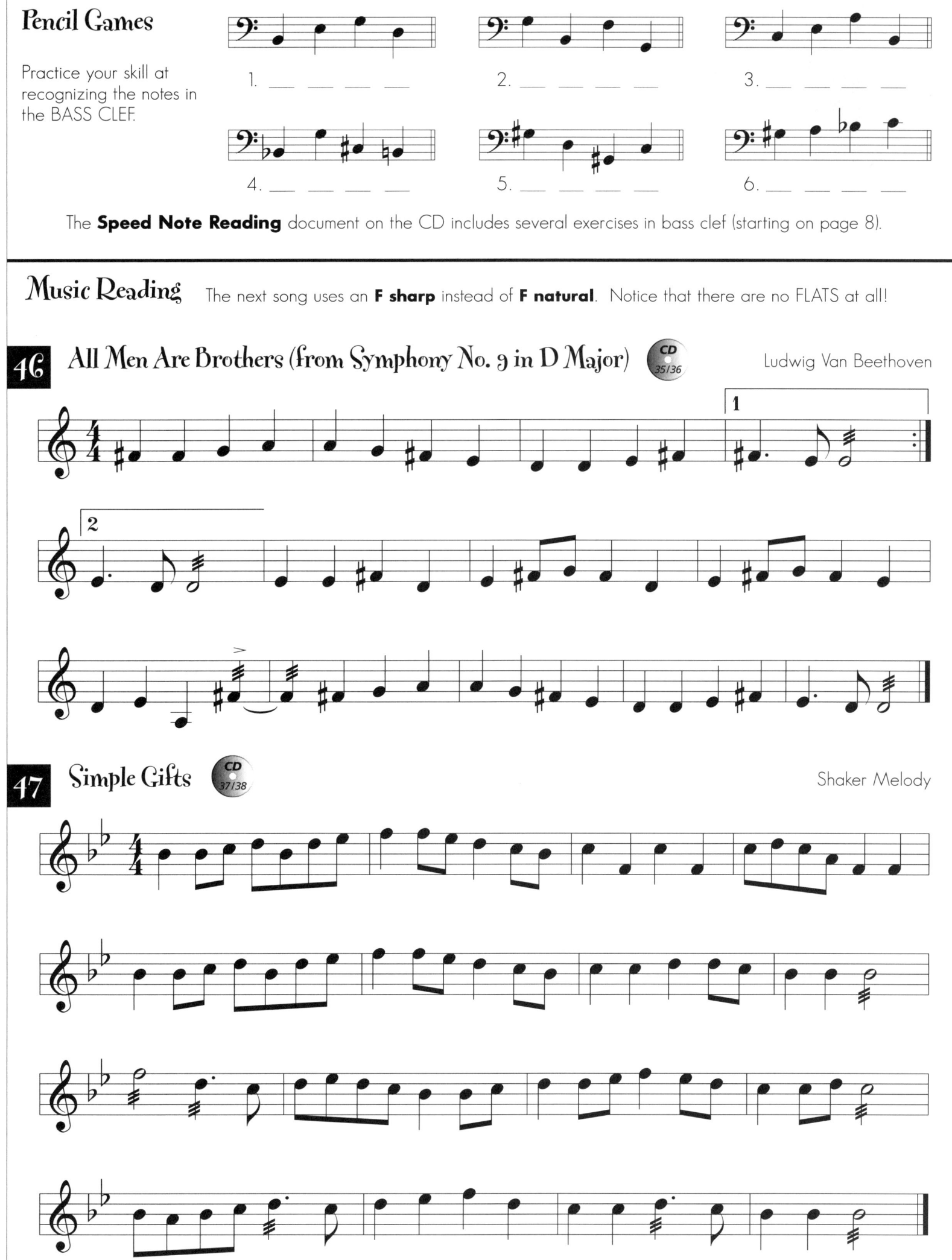

Syncopation   Music Theory

In modern dance music, notes on the weak beats (2 & 4, or the "upbeat") are often emphasized (or <u>accented</u>) for effect. These syncopated rhythms are especially present in **jazz** music. Write the counts under the notes in these two lines, then see if you can clap while you count out loud to a metronome. Try not to "swing" the rhythm until you can perform it "straight" PERFECTLY!

Music Reading

Not only does this next song have several syncopated rhythms, but it also has a few accidentals thrown in for good measure. Watch your key signature, and remember the rule: an accidental returns to the key signature note when you pass the bar line!

48 *Keyboard Boogie*

49 *Reveille*   Traditional

Now that you are used to reading a few sharps, try this one on for size! Don't memorize – keep your eyes on the music!

Dynamic Markings and Musical Terms —memorize each of these musical terms.

f	**FORTE**	loud				
mf	**MEZZO FORTE**	medium loud	*cresc*	**CRESCENDO**	gradually get louder
p	**PIANO**	soft	*accel*	**ACCELERANDO**	gradually get faster

Music Theory

Music Reading

The short "Russian Dance" starts slow and soft, and gradually builds to an exciting finish by using the **crescendo** and **accelerando**. Watch the dynamics and accents very carefully!

50 Russian Sailor's Dance Reinhold Gliere

p – 1st X
f – 2nd X
gradual cresc. and accelerando to the end

51 Turkey in the Straw Traditional

Sixteenth Notes   *Music Theory*

A sixteenth note has two flags (remember that the 8th note has one). There are TWO sixteenth notes in each 8th note or FOUR sixteenth's in each quarter note.

Draw in the bar lines in the following examples, then write the counting under the notes. Clap and count each line.

①

②

Music Reading

Always use an alternating sticking when playing 16th notes on the keyboard. Start slowly on this etude, and gradually work it up to a faster tempo. Remember to check the key signature!

52

Tempo Terms —These terms are used to describe the speed of the music.   *Music Theory*

Largo	*Andante*	*Moderato*	*Allegro*	*Presto*
Very Slow		Medium		Very Fast

Speed Test

This Speed test is a little more difficult because it uses flats AND sharps. Since there is no key signature, any note without an accidental is automatically NATURAL.

32

Write the note names under the notes in the following exercises.

Speed Test

① ② ③

④ ⑤ ⑥

Special Solo — This solo is very difficult and can be used as a "show off" piece at solo contest or concerts! Alternate as much as possible and strive to keep your eyes on the music!

53 Excerpt from "William Tell Overture" — Rossini

Allegro

33

Lesson 16

Music Theory

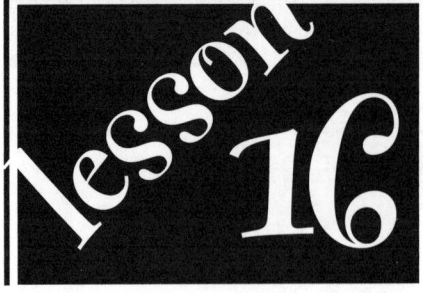

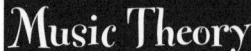

This is the final stage before we start reading MUSIC in bass clef!

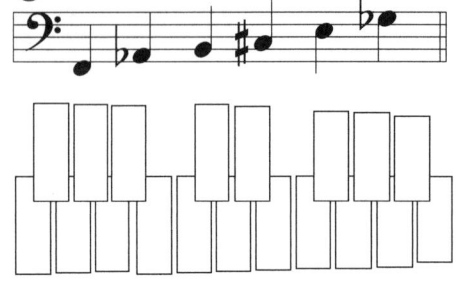

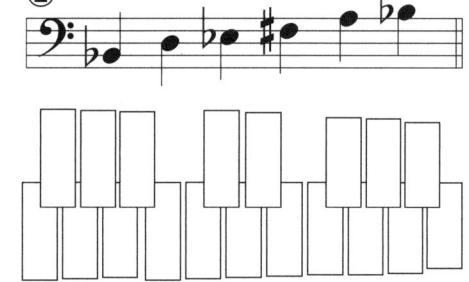

Time yourself on each line to see who is the fastest in the class!

①

②

③

④

⑤

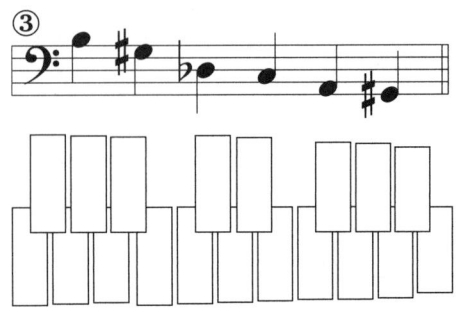

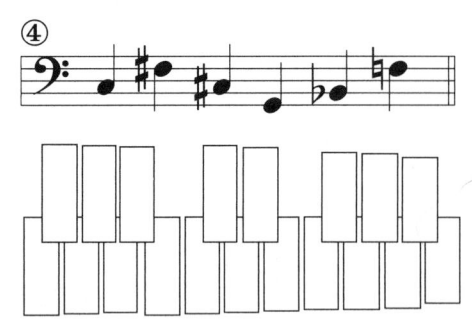

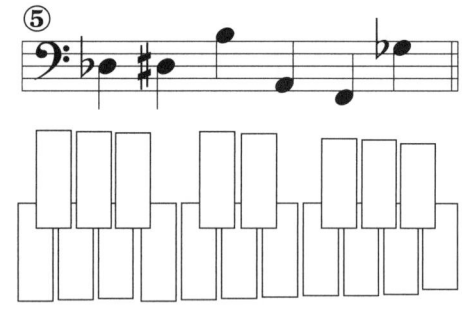

Music Reading

Some of the rolls in this piece are connected with **SLURS**. When playing a **slur**, try not to leave any space between the roll and the following note. Good luck with your first piece in bass clef!

54

Allegro

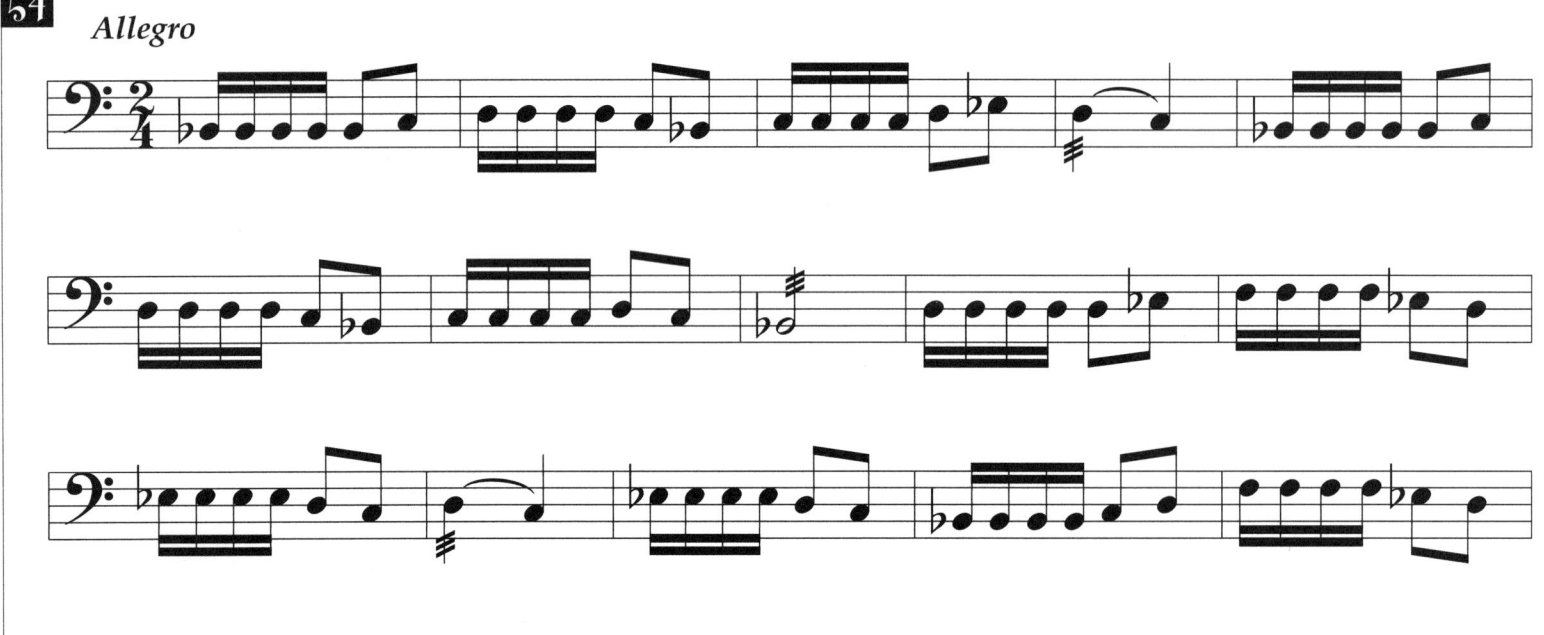

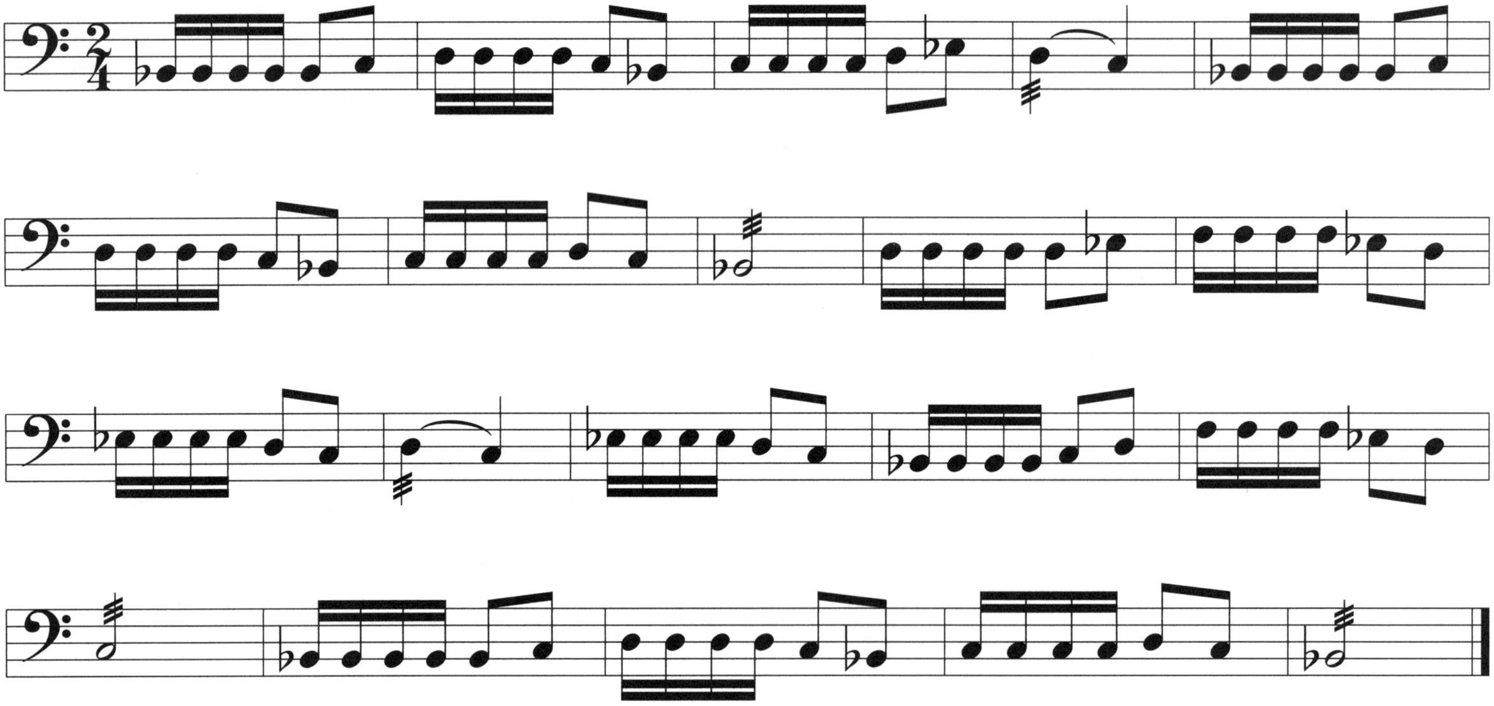

Speed Test

This Speed Test is even more difficult to play because it uses a key signature with three sharps. You may NOT write in the accidentals in front of the notes affected by the key signature!

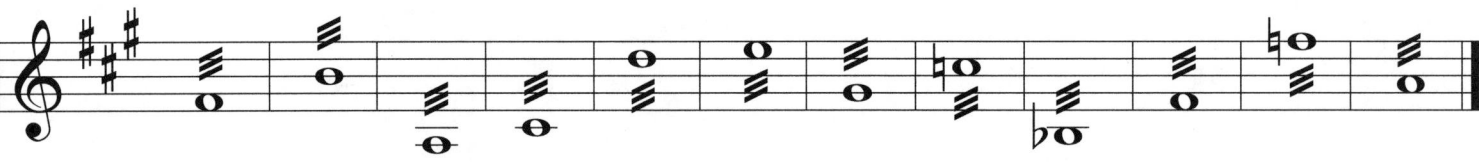

55 — Speed Test

This short excerpt from Dvorak's Largo from Symphony #9 contains a **D.C. al Fine**. Simply repeat back to the beginning (Da Capo), and play until you reach the Fine ("fee-nay" or finish).

Special Solo — This song includes a *crescendo* (< - which means to gradually get louder), a *diminuendo* (> - gradually get softer), and a *ritardando* (ritard - gradually get slower).

56 Hunter's Chorus — von Weber

Moderato

ritard

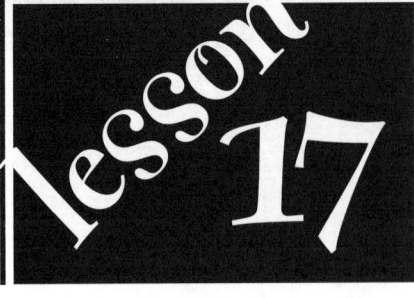

INTERVALS

Music Theory

Intervals in music are used to describe the distance between two notes. Use the starting note to count up to the next pitch. The number that you get is the interval.

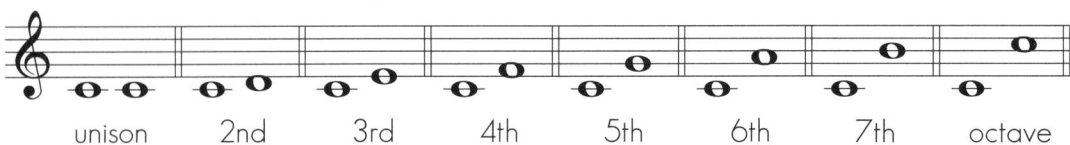

Draw a whole note above or below (indicated by the arrows) on the correct **interval** from the starting pitch given.

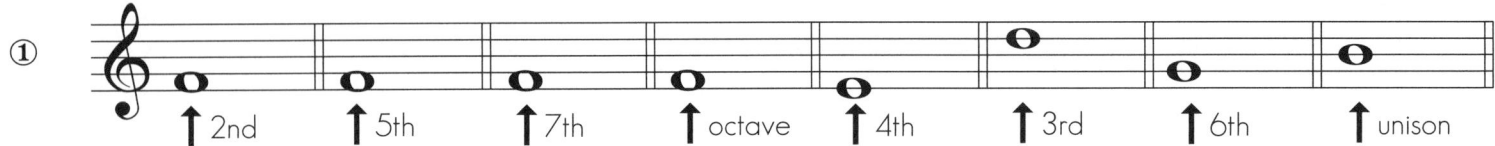

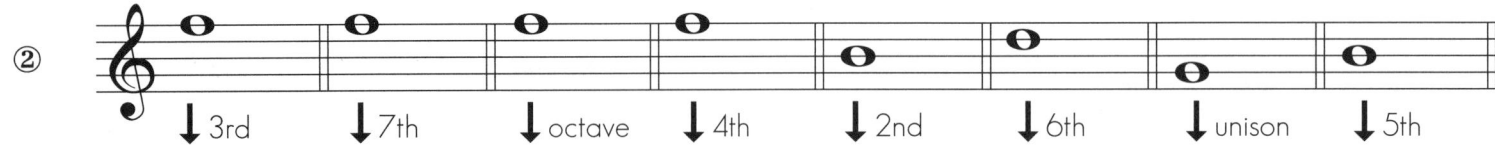

Music Reading

This version of Dussek's "Old Dance" is written in BASS CLEF. Play this song as low on your keyboard as possible (the note A is the lowest note in this song).

57 *Moderato*

This Speed Test is written in bass clef. Remember that the OCTAVE that you play is important!

Speed Test

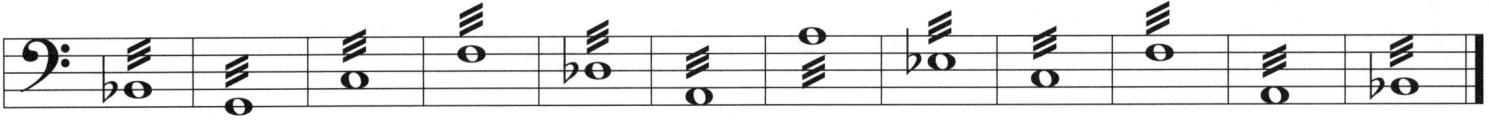

Speed Test

Fill in the blanks with the correct note names. Remember the accidental rule: an accidental (in this a natural), remains in effect for the entire measure and the bar line reinstates the key signature!

Special Solo

This solo is very difficult to learn at first, but with work it will be worth the effort! Try to learn one section at a time. Write in the stickings that your teacher suggests, and DON'T MEMORIZE!

58 Orpheus in the Underworld — Offenbach

Lesson 18

Music Theory

Dotted Eighth Notes

Remember that a dot behind a note INCREASES ITS VALUE BY HALF of its original value. Since one 8th note equals two 16th's, a **dotted eighth note** would equal THREE 16th's:

After you write in the counts under the notes, clap and count these exercises out loud to a metronome.

Music Reading

Start slow and **subdivide** the dotted eighth notes (count the first three 16th's out loud).

59. Battle Hymn of the Republic — Traditional

Moderato

Speed Test

This Speed Test is written in treble clef. Check the key signature before you begin.

Fill in the blanks with the correct note names. This exercise is in bass clef and even includes a key signature. Remember the rules for accidentals!

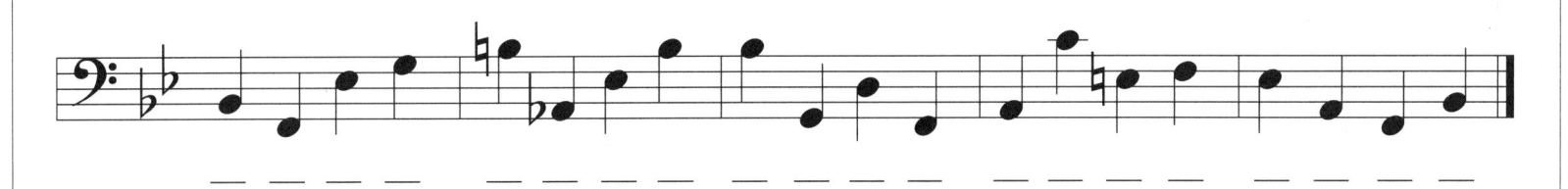

Speed Test

Music Reading
Schumann's "Soldier's March" includes double stops as well as several tricky dynamics. Start slow and gradually work to a march tempo.

60 Burlesque — L. Mozart

Allegro

f ± p

f ... *p*

f ... *ritard*

61 Soldier's March — R. Schumann

mf ... *p* ... *mf*

p ... *f* ... *p*

f ... *p* ... *f*

p ... *f*

Lesson 19

Music Theory

"Eight" Time Signatures $\frac{3}{8}$ $\frac{6}{8}$ $\frac{9}{8}$

When a time signature has an '8' on the bottom, you would beat time to the 8th note. In this example, there are 3 beats to a measure and the 8th note gets one beat.

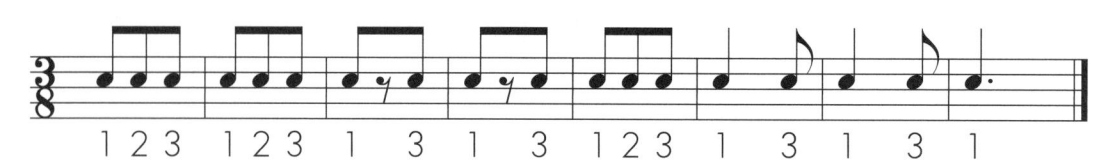

1 2 3   1 2 3   1   3   1   3   1 2 3   1   3   1   3   1

You may want to beat time to the **dotted quarter** in these exercises (where 3 eighth notes receive one beat).

①

②

Music Reading

Start with the left hand and alternate throughout (you may want to use "double strokes" in the first two measures of the last line). Work up to TWO beats per measure (dotted quarter gets the beat).

62 Irish Washerwoman   Irish Jig

Allegro

Speed Test

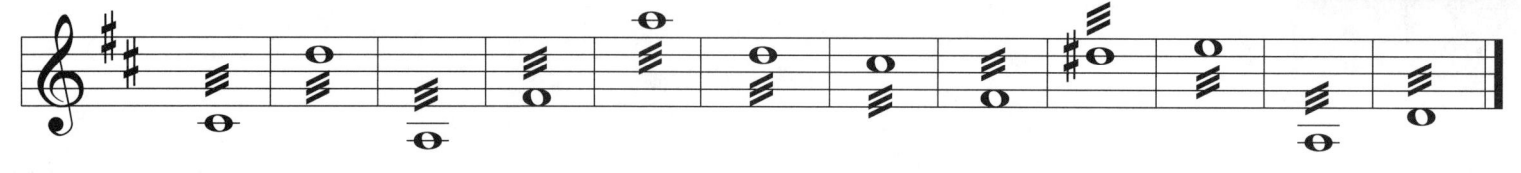

This Speed Test is written in treble clef. Check the key signature before you begin.

Music Reading

Bach's "Joy" is meant to be played "**expressivo**" (with expression). While there are dynamics suggested, feel free to make up your own dynamics to fit your own mood and musicality.

63. Jesu, Joy of Man's Desire — Bach

Adagio Expressivo
mp
cresc.
diminuendo al fine *rit.*

64. The Sorcerer's Apprentice — Paul Dukas

f *p*
mf
p *f*
p
f

Lesson 20

Cut Time ¢

Music Theory

In "**Cut Time**," the player beats time to the HALF NOTE. Half notes fall on the downbeats (like quarter notes in quarter time), quarters fall on the upbeats (like 8th notes in quarter time), etc. Write in the counting under this line, then clap and count it out loud to a metronome.

Music Reading

The next two songs include a new tempo marking. *Allegretto* is not quite as fast as *Allegro*, but faster than *Andante*.

65 Arkansas Traveler — Traditional

Allegretto

66 Gavotte — J.S. Bach

Allegretto

p ... *mf* ... *dim.*

p ... *mf* — **Fine**

mp

D.C. al Fine

Special Solo

Congratulations, you've made it to the end of the book! Once you have it worked up, this Sonatina makes a nice performance piece for a solo festival with the accompaniment MP3.

67. Sonatina — Clementi

Moderato

mf

mp ... *f*

p

cresc.

mf

f

ritard

Appendix: Lesson One

Pencil Game: Draw one of each of the following on the staff provided:

| Treble Clef | Bar Line | Time Signature | Double Bar Line | Quarter Note |

Pencil Game: Fill in the blanks to show your knowledge of the musical alphabet (UP the alphabet and DOWN the alphabet).

FORWARDS:

① A _ _ _ _ _   ② F _ _ _ _ _   ③ C _ _ _ _ _

BACKWARDS:

④ A _ _ _ _ _   ⑤ F _ _ _ _ _   ⑥ C _ _ _ _ _

Speed Test: DO NOT write the names under the notes! Instead, set a metronome on 60 beats per minute and say the note names out loud to every 2nd click. As you get faster at naming the notes, speed the metronome up.

Speed Test #2: Use the musical alphabet to find the note on the keyboard. The note "**F**," which is provided for you, is the first natural key BELOW the group of three accidentals.

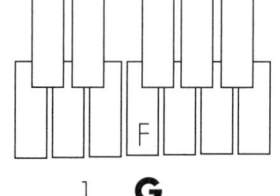

1. **G** 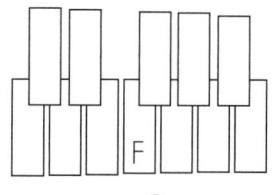   2. **C** 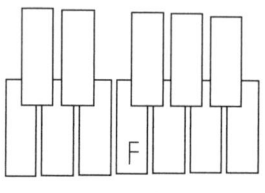   3. **A** 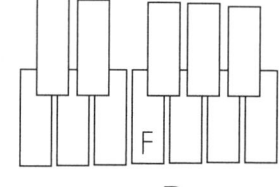   4. **D** 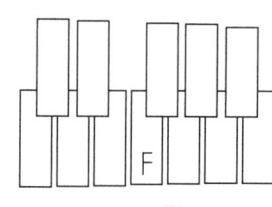   5. **B**

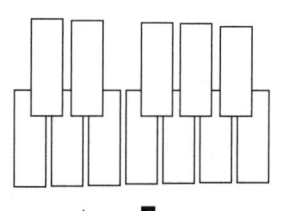

6. **E** 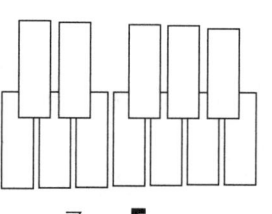   7. **F** 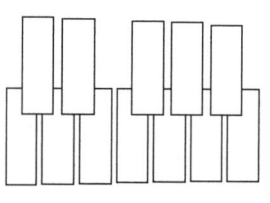   8. **D** 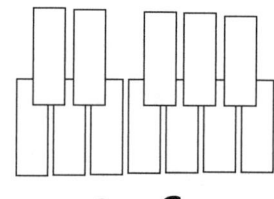   9. **C** 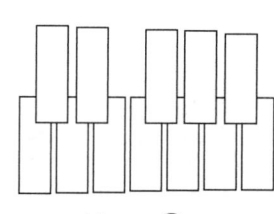   10. **G**

44

Appendix: Lesson Two

Speed Test #1: Set a metronome on 80 beats per minute and say the note names to every 2nd click.

Speed Test #2: Put an "**X**" on the note that is DOWN a half step from the note indicated.

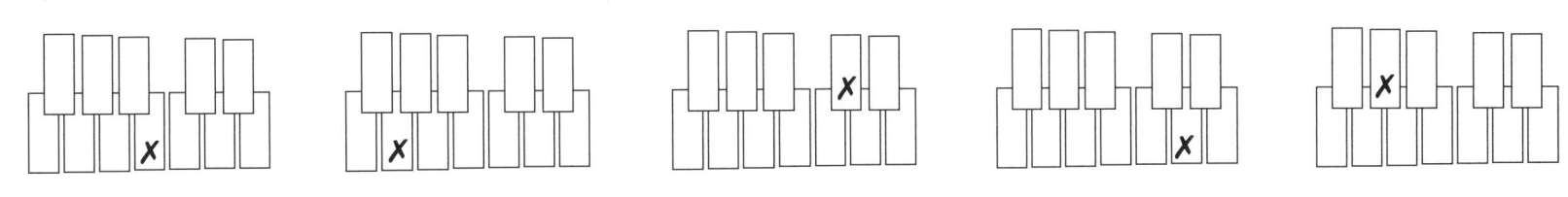

Speed Test #3: Remember that a **Flat** lowers a pitch one half step. Find the FLAT note on the keyboard below.

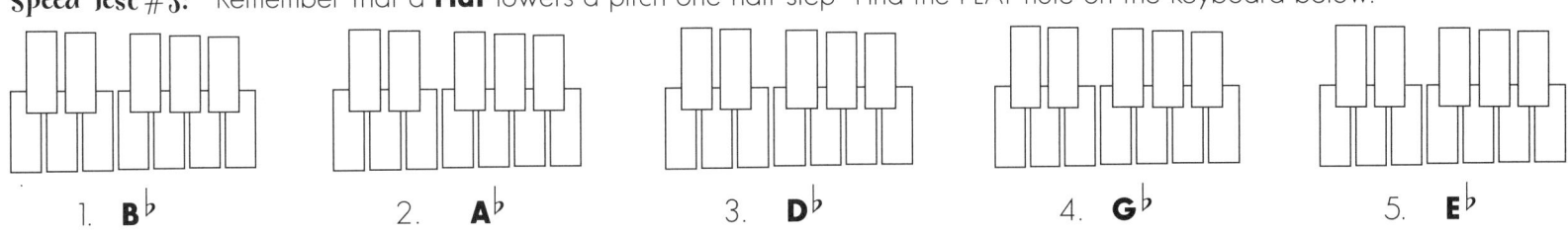

1. B♭   2. A♭   3. D♭   4. G♭   5. E♭

Music Reading: Before you attempt to play these lines, say the note names out loud while you "finger-through" each one.

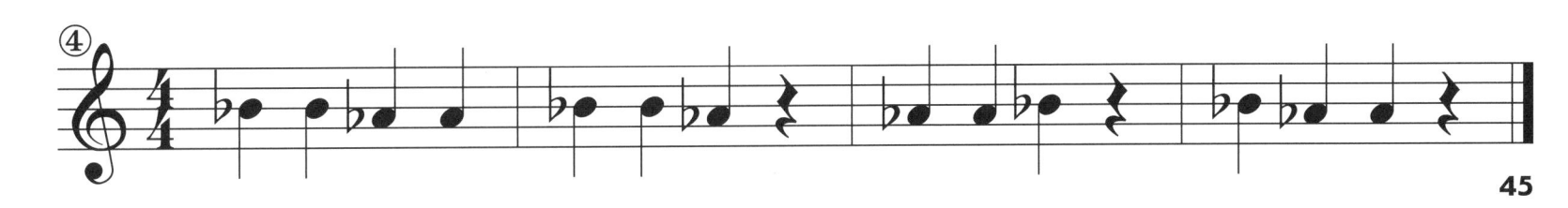

Appendix: Lesson Three

Speed Test #1: Set a metronome on 60 beats per minute and say the note names to every click. Who in your class can say the note names the fastest without making a mistake (while keeping in tempo with the metronome)?

Speed Test #2: The note "**F**" is the 1st natural below the group of three accidentals. Find the correct note on the keyboard.

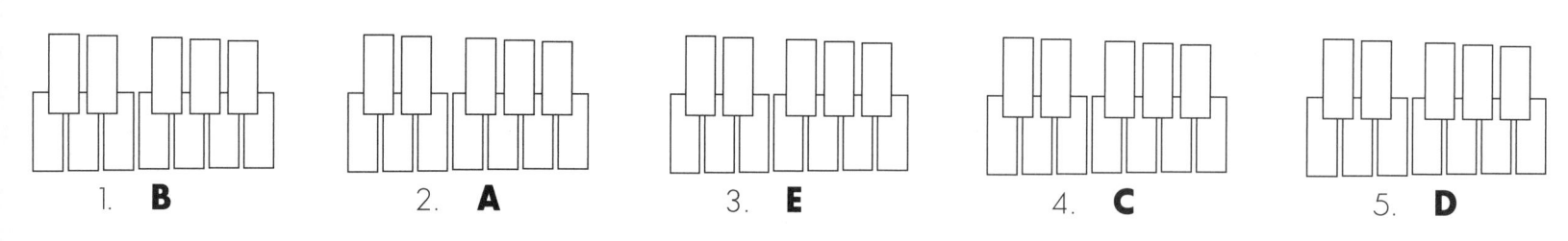

1. **B** 2. **A** 3. **E** 4. **C** 5. **D**

Speed Test #3: Remember that a **Flat** lowers a pitch one half step. Find the FLAT note on the keyboard below.

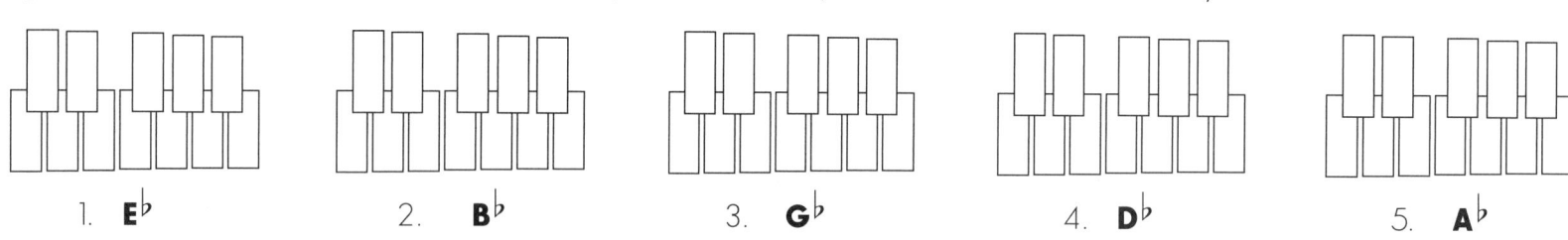

1. **E♭** 2. **B♭** 3. **G♭** 4. **D♭** 5. **A♭**

Music Reading: "Finger-through" and say the note names out loud BEFORE you attempt to play these lines!

46

Speed Test #4: Set a metronome on 60 beats per minute and say the note names to every click. Who in your class can say the note names the fastest without making a mistake?

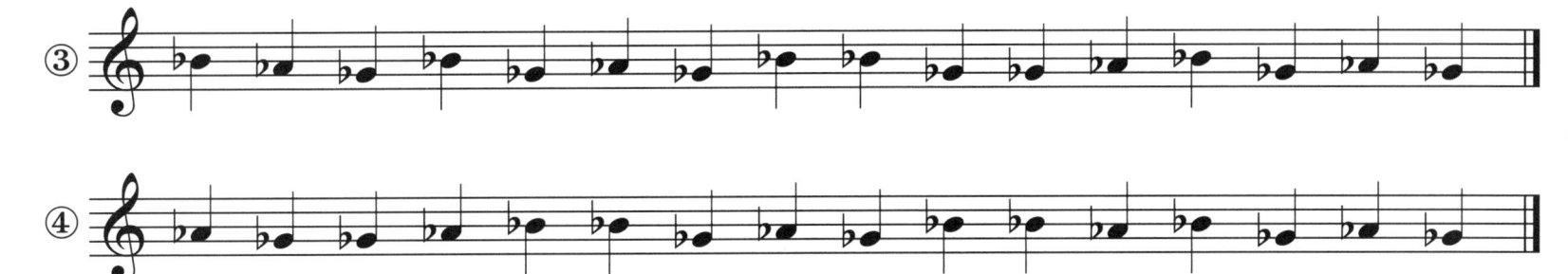

Speed Test #5: Put an "x" on the note that is up or down a WHOLE STEP from the note give as indicated by the arrows. Remember that a whole step is equal to *two* half steps.

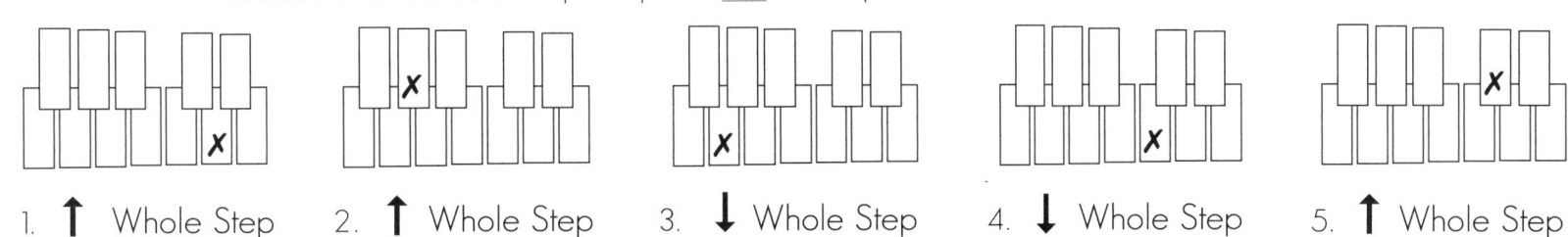

1. ↑ Whole Step 2. ↑ Whole Step 3. ↓ Whole Step 4. ↓ Whole Step 5. ↑ Whole Step

Speed Test #6: Find TWO notes on each keyboard. The first note is a NATURAL, the second is an ACCIDENTAL.

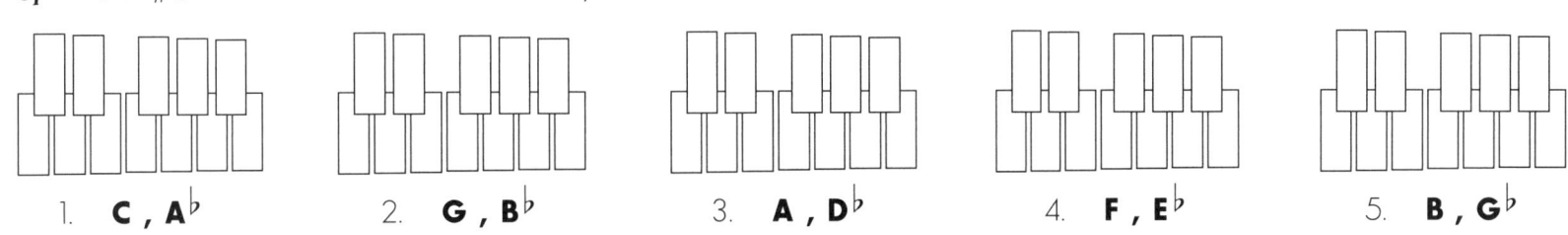

1. **C, A♭** 2. **G, B♭** 3. **A, D♭** 4. **F, E♭** 5. **B, G♭**

Music Reading: Never write note names in your music — you'll wind up looking at what you wrote instead of the music!

Appendix: Lesson Four

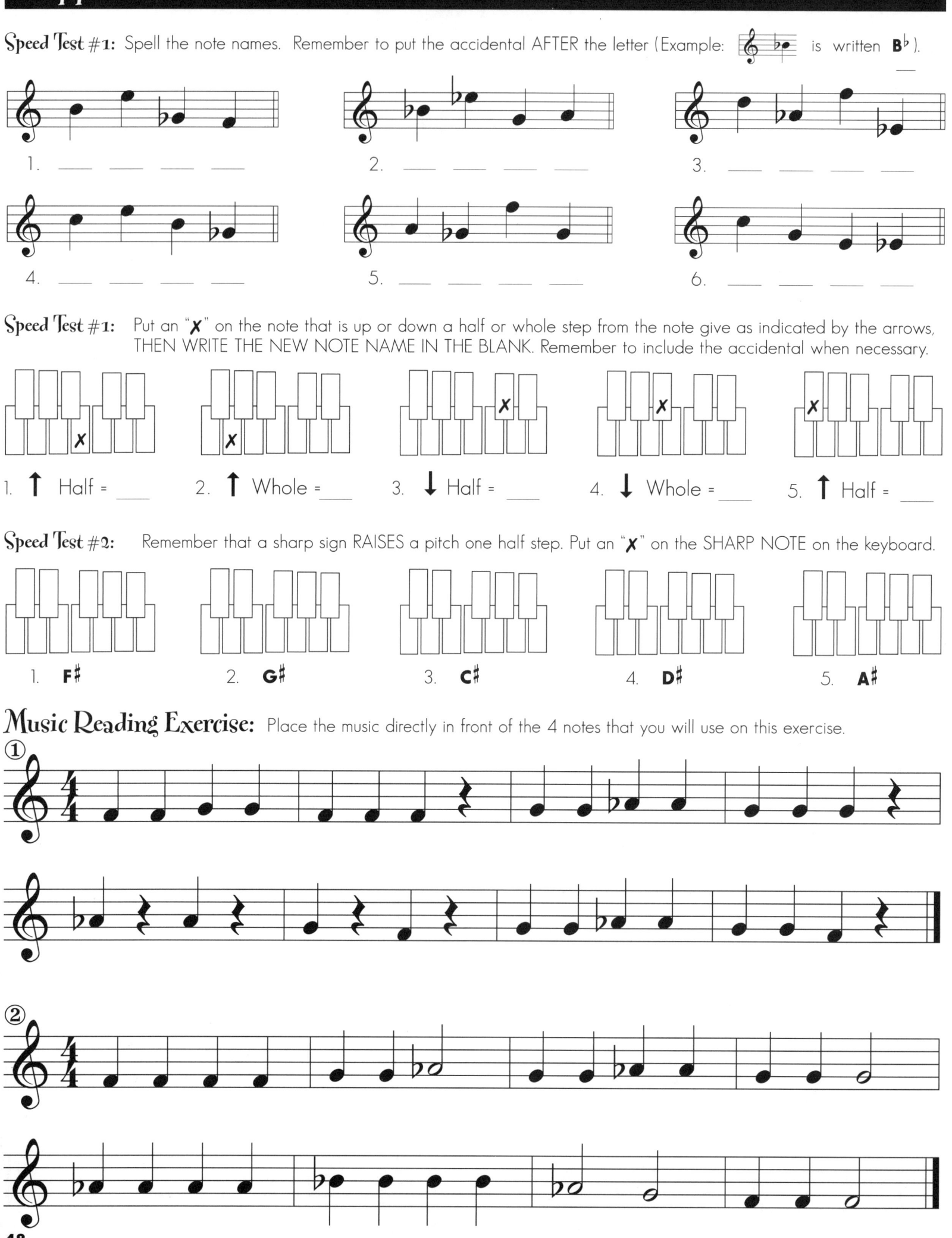

Speed Test #1: Spell the note names. Remember to put the accidental AFTER the letter (Example: ♭𝅗𝅥 is written **B♭**).

1. _____   2. _____   3. _____

4. _____   5. _____   6. _____

Speed Test #1: Put an "**✗**" on the note that is up or down a half or whole step from the note give as indicated by the arrows, THEN WRITE THE NEW NOTE NAME IN THE BLANK. Remember to include the accidental when necessary.

1. ↑ Half = ___   2. ↑ Whole = ___   3. ↓ Half = ___   4. ↓ Whole = ___   5. ↑ Half = ___

Speed Test #2: Remember that a sharp sign RAISES a pitch one half step. Put an "**✗**" on the SHARP NOTE on the keyboard.

1. **F♯**   2. **G♯**   3. **C♯**   4. **D♯**   5. **A♯**

Music Reading Exercise: Place the music directly in front of the 4 notes that you will use on this exercise.

①

②

48

Speed Test #5: Set a metronome on 80 beats per minute and say the note names to every click. Each day, speed up the metronome by 10 beats per minute!

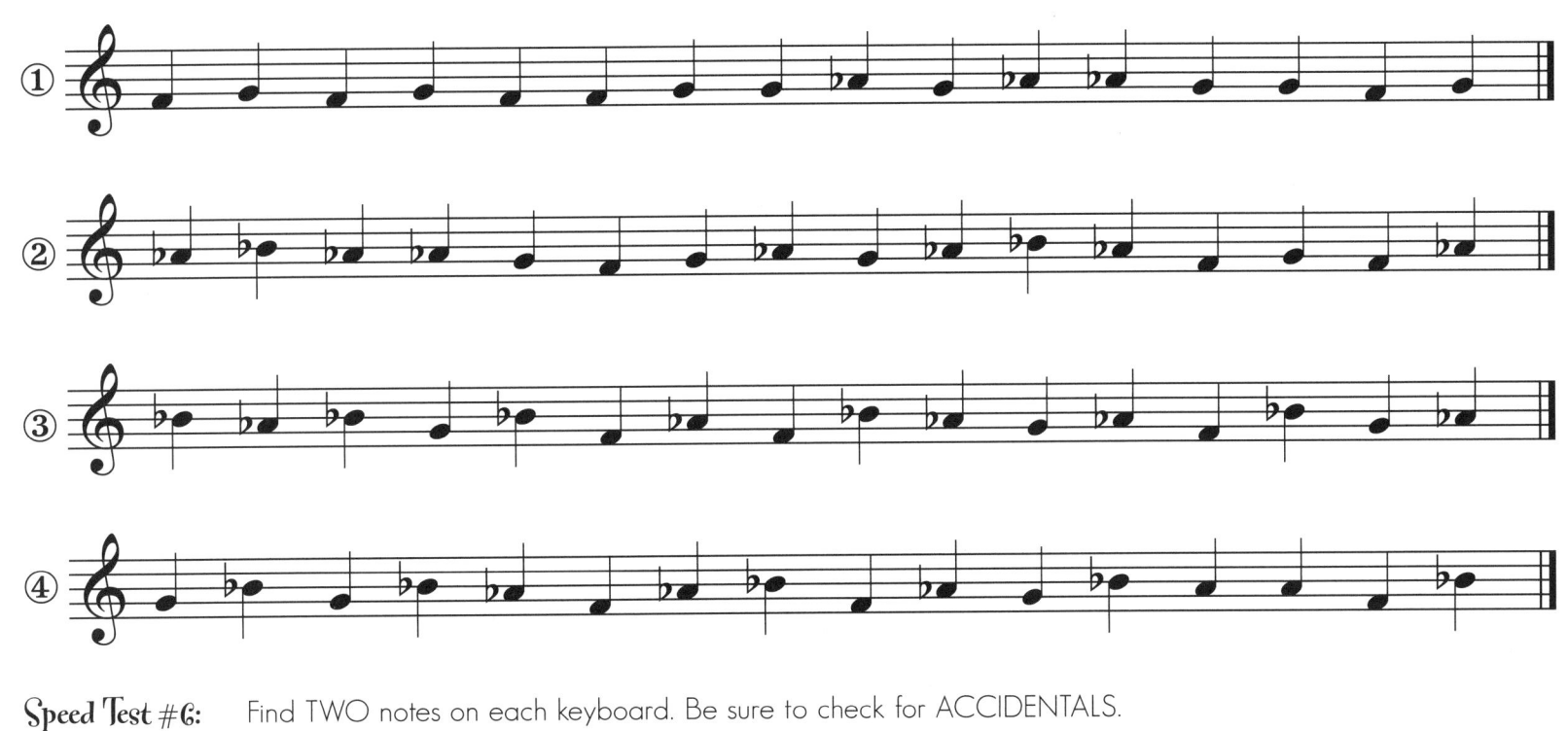

Speed Test #6: Find TWO notes on each keyboard. Be sure to check for ACCIDENTALS.

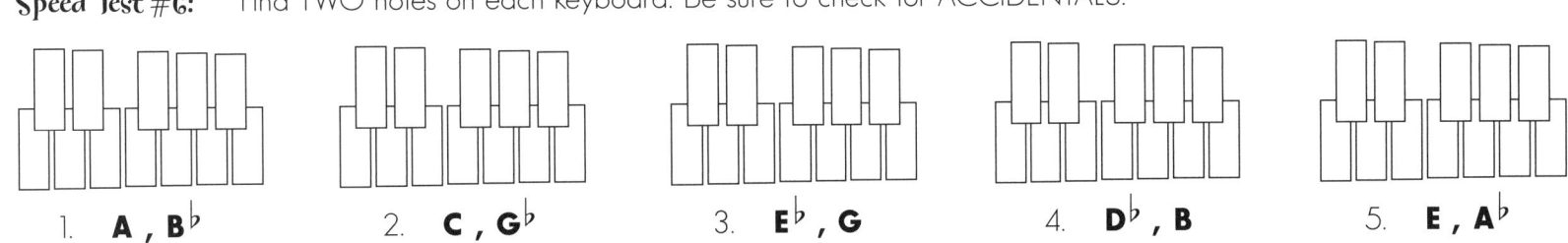

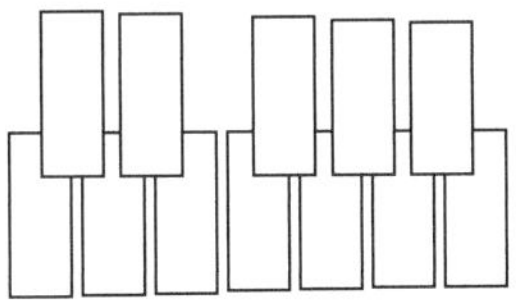

1. **A , B♭**   2. **C , G♭**   3. **E♭ , G**   4. **D♭ , B**   5. **E , A♭**

Music Reading Exercise: Always keep your eyes on your music! Use your peripheral vision to see the keyboard.

Appendix: Lesson Five

Speed Test #1: Spell the note names in the blanks provided.

1. ___ ___ ___ ___ ___
2. ___ ___ ___ ___ ___
3. ___ ___ ___ ___ ___

Speed Test #2: Put an "✗" on the correct notes on the keyboard. Remember that a SHARP <u>raises</u> the pitch of a note one half step and a FLAT <u>lowers</u> the pitch of a note one half step.

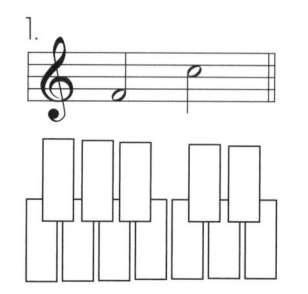

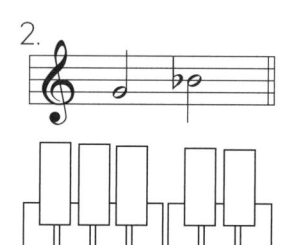

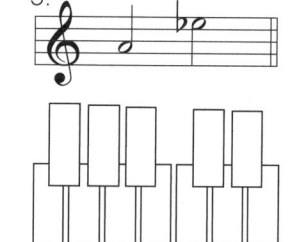

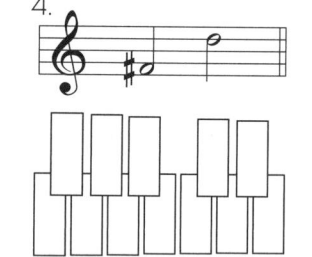

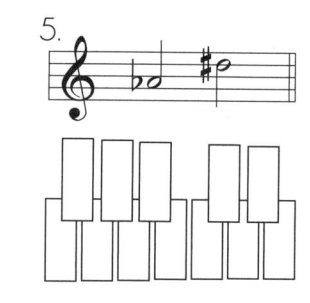

Music Reading Exercise:

①

②

50

Speed Test #3: Set a metronome on 80 beats per minute and say the note names to every click. Each day, speed up the metronome by 10 beats per minute!

Speed Test #4: Write the **name** of the notes on the correct keys on the keyboard.

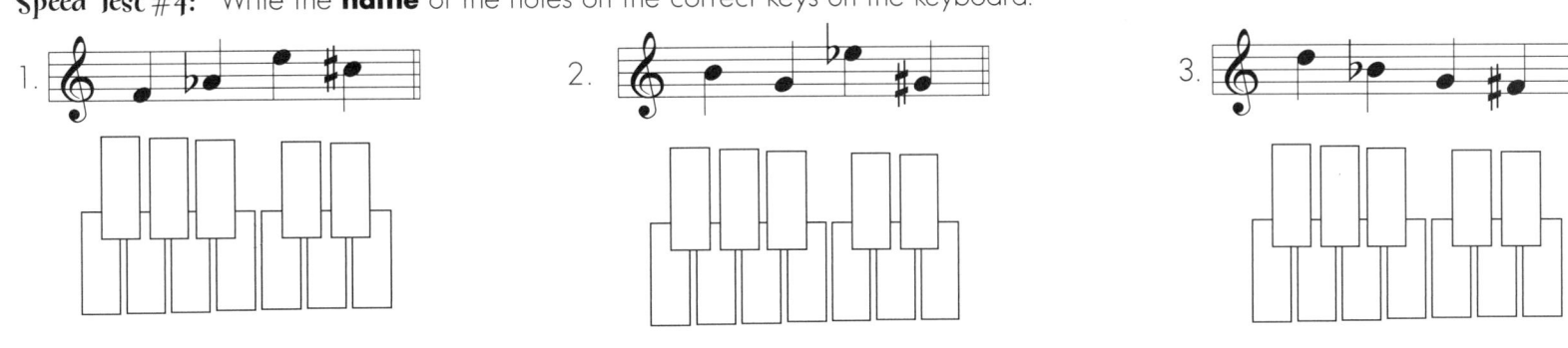

Speed Test #5: Given the starting pitch, build the remaining four notes of the tetrachord. Remember that a tetrachord has the pattern of **whole step, whole step, half step**.

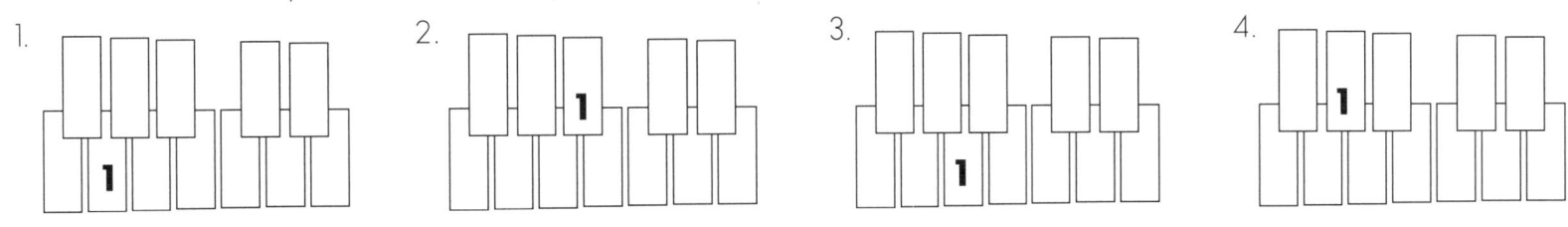

Music Reading Exercise:

Appendix: Lesson Six

Speed Test #1: Use the musical alphabet to "count" up or down the ledger lines to find the notes in these exercises.

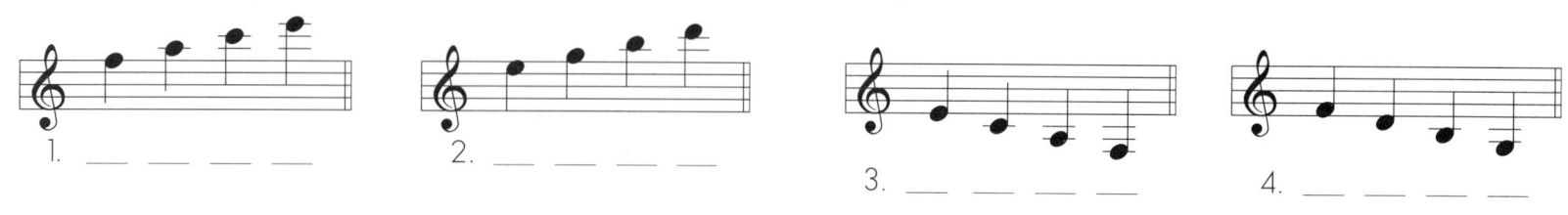

1. __ __ __ __ __
2. __ __ __ __ __
3. __ __ __ __ __
4. __ __ __ __ __

Speed Test #2: Say the note names out loud to a metronome set on "80".

Music Reading Exercises: Finger through each of these exercises before you play them on the keyboard.

Speed Test #3: Say the note names out loud to a metronome set on "80".

Speed Test #4: Draw in the bar lines and write the counting under the notes. Clap and count out loud to a metronome.

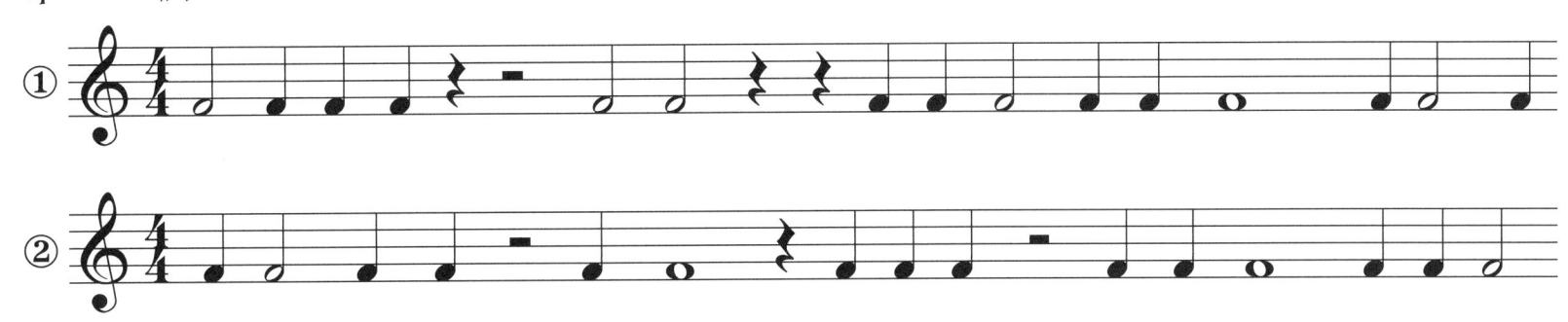

Music Reading Exercises:
Finger through each of these exercises before you play them on the keyboard.

Appendix: Lesson Seven

Speed Test #1: Build the remaining 4 notes of the tetrachord, then put the correct **accidentals** in the box next to the note names. If the note is <u>natural</u>, leave the box blank. The first example has been done for you.

1. A♭ B♭ C☐ D♭
2. B☐ C☐ D☐ E☐
3. F☐ G☐ A☐ B☐
4. A☐ B☐ C☐ D☐
5. E☐ F☐ G☐ A☐
6. C☐ D☐ E☐ F☐
7. D☐ E☐ F☐ G☐
8. E☐ F☐ G☐ A☐

Music Reading Exercises: Finger through each of these exercises before you play them on the keyboard.

54

Speed Test #2: Pay attention to the KEY SIGNATURE as you read these lines out loud to a metronome.

Music Reading Exercises: Finger through each of these exercises before you play them on the keyboard.

Appendix: Lesson Eight

Speed Test #1: Write the names of the accidentals that appear in these **key signatures**.

1. ___ 2. ___ 3. ___ ___ 4. ___ ___ 5. ___ ___ ___

Speed Test #2: Draw a **flat** or **sharp** in front of the affected notes by using the **key signatures** in the following examples, then write the note names under the notes. The first measure has been done for you.

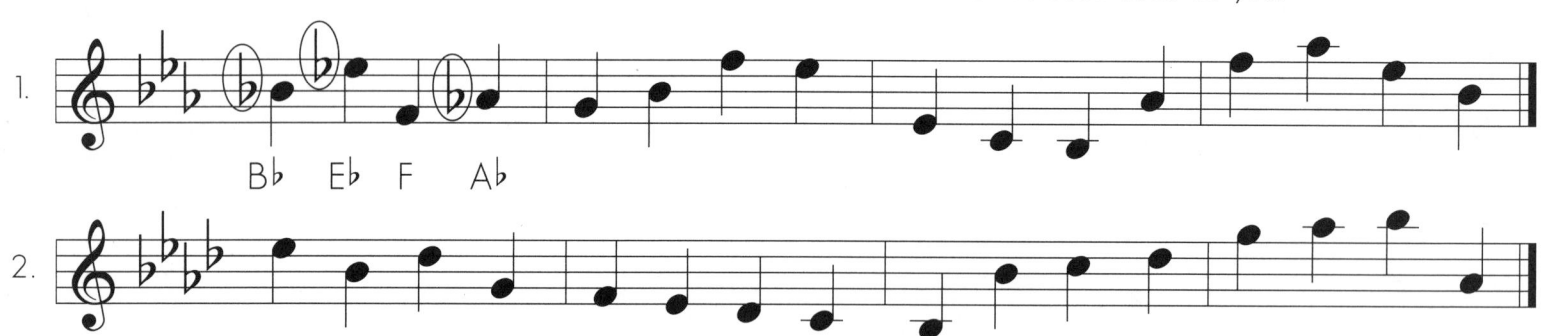

1. Bb Eb F Ab

2.

Music Reading Exercises

①

②

56

Speed Test #3: Say the note names out loud to a metronome. For a difficult challenge, try fingering through the lines as well!

Music Reading Exercises

Appendix: Lesson Nine

Speed Test #1: Write the names of the notes on the correct keys on the keyboard. Check the **key signature** on each line before you begin!

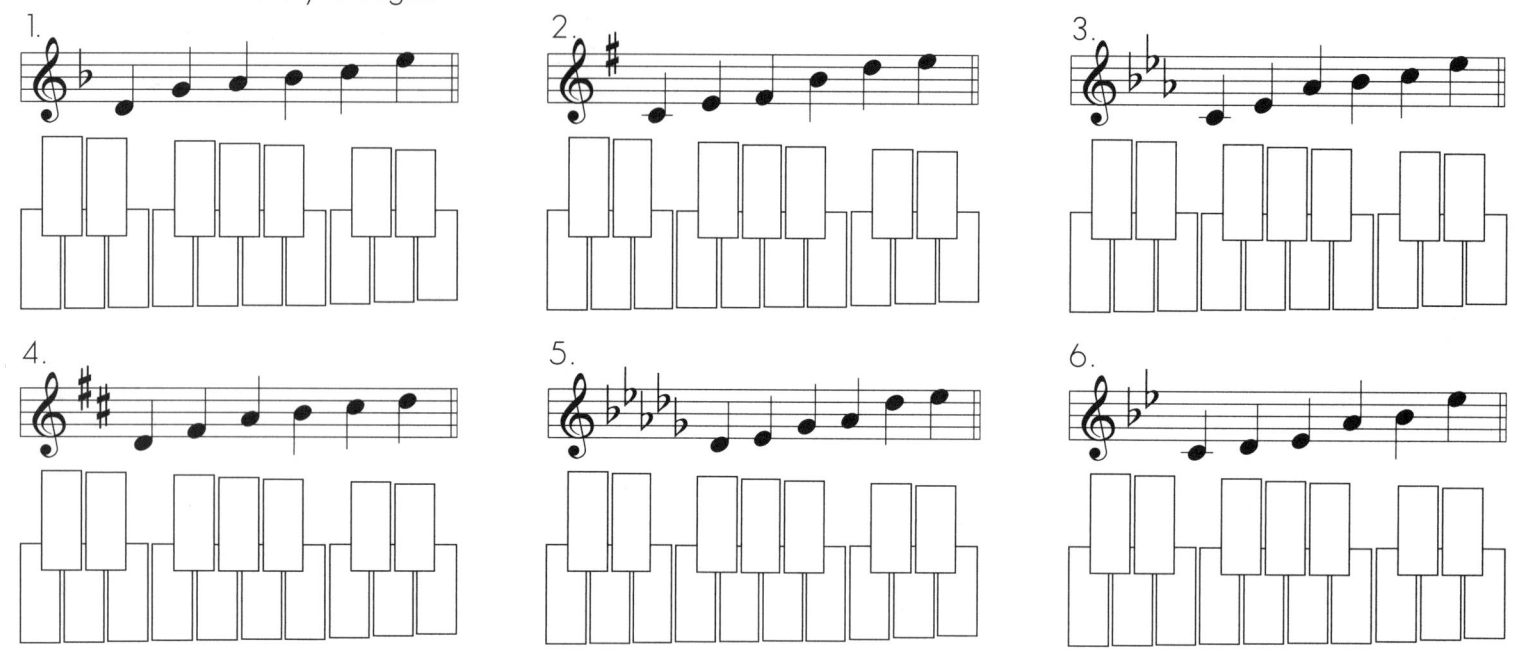

Music Reading Exercises:

Speed Test #2:   Always keep your eyes moving forward. Work with a metronome to keep you honest!

Music Reading Exercises:

Appendix: Lesson Ten

Speed Test #1: Write the names of the notes on the correct key on the keyboard. Check the key signature on each line!

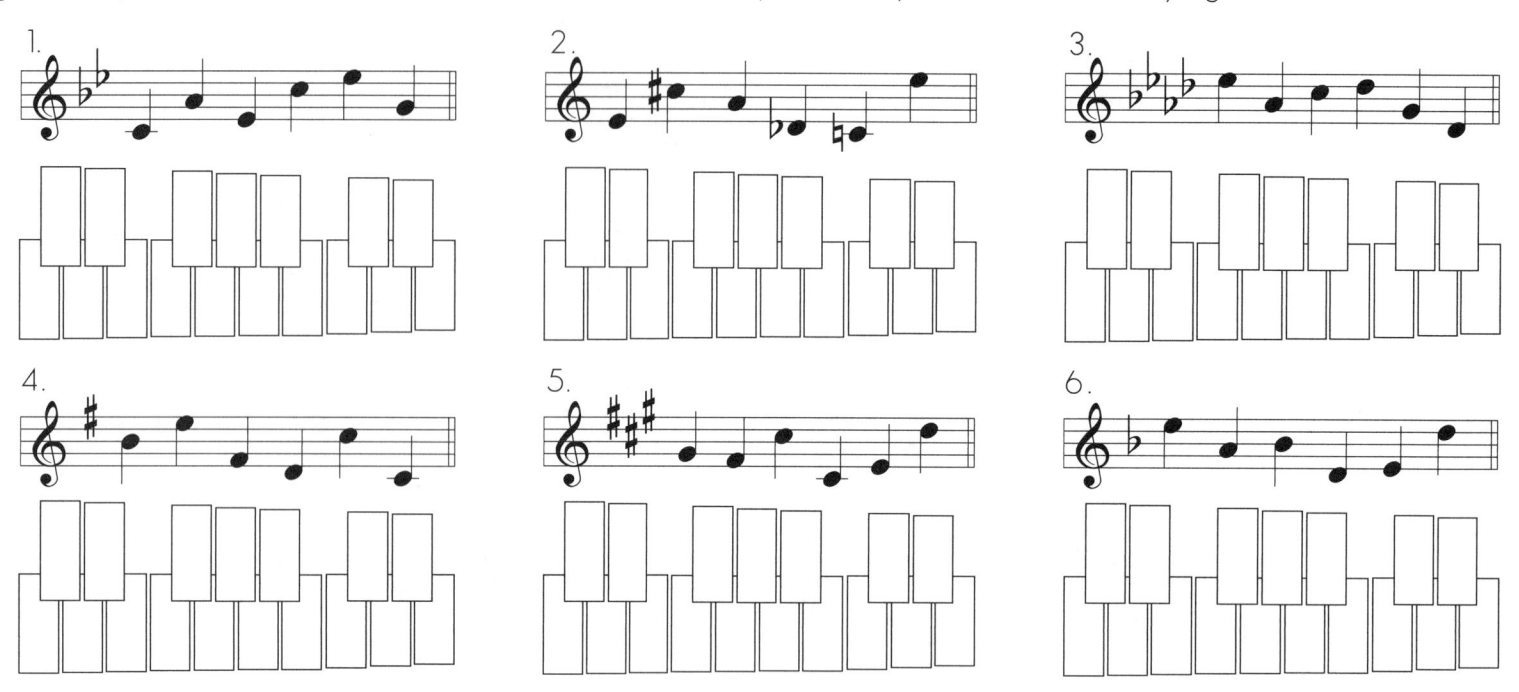

Music Reading Exercises: Your teacher may want you to use a "double-sticking" for repeated 8th notes in line #2.

Speed Test #2: Start slow and work with a metronome until you can say all the note names without mistakes – then speed up.

Music Reading Exercises:

Appendix: Lesson Eleven

Speed Test #1: Using the starting notes below, build the remaining 4 notes of the tetrachord, then spell the tetrachord in the blanks provided. Remember to include the accidentals where necessary.

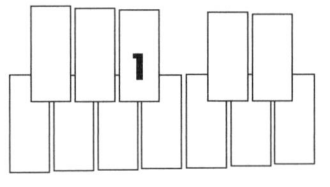

1. **B♭** ___ ___ ___
2. **G** ___ ___ ___ 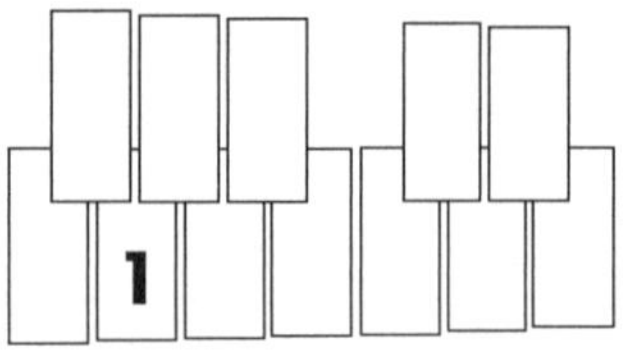
3. **A♭** ___ ___ ___ 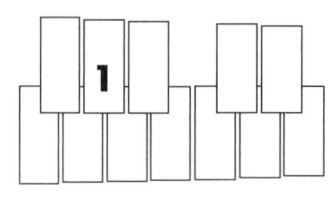
4. **B** ___ ___ ___ 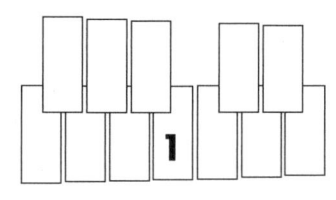
5. **D♭** ___ ___ ___ 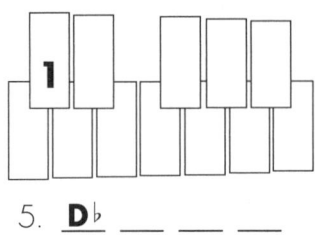
6. **E** ___ ___ ___ 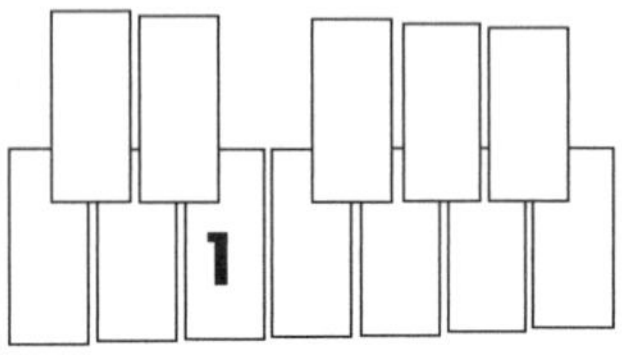
7. **E♭** ___ ___ ___ 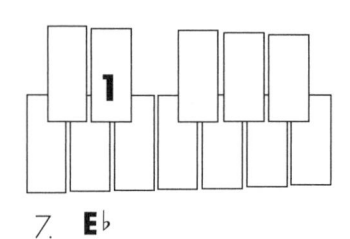
8. **D** ___ ___ ___ 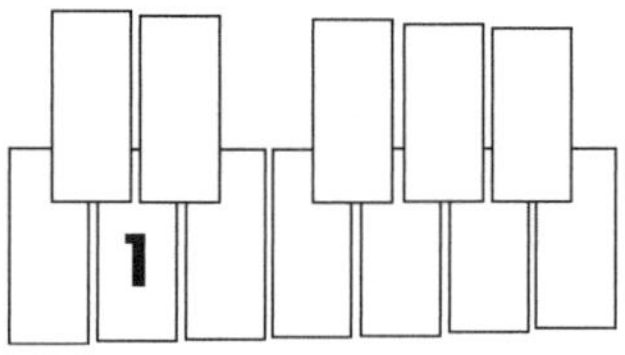

Speed Test #2: Write the names of the notes in the blanks provided. Remember to check the key signature!

Music Reading Exercises:

Duet for two players

Work each part up separately with a metronome. If playing on a xylophone or marimba, you may wish to roll half and whole notes (though I don't recommend it on the bells).

Appendix: Lesson Twelve

Speed Test #1: Write the note names on the correct key on the keyboard. Remember, you can also use the SPEED NOTE READING TUTOR video game on the CD to further improve your speed reading ability.

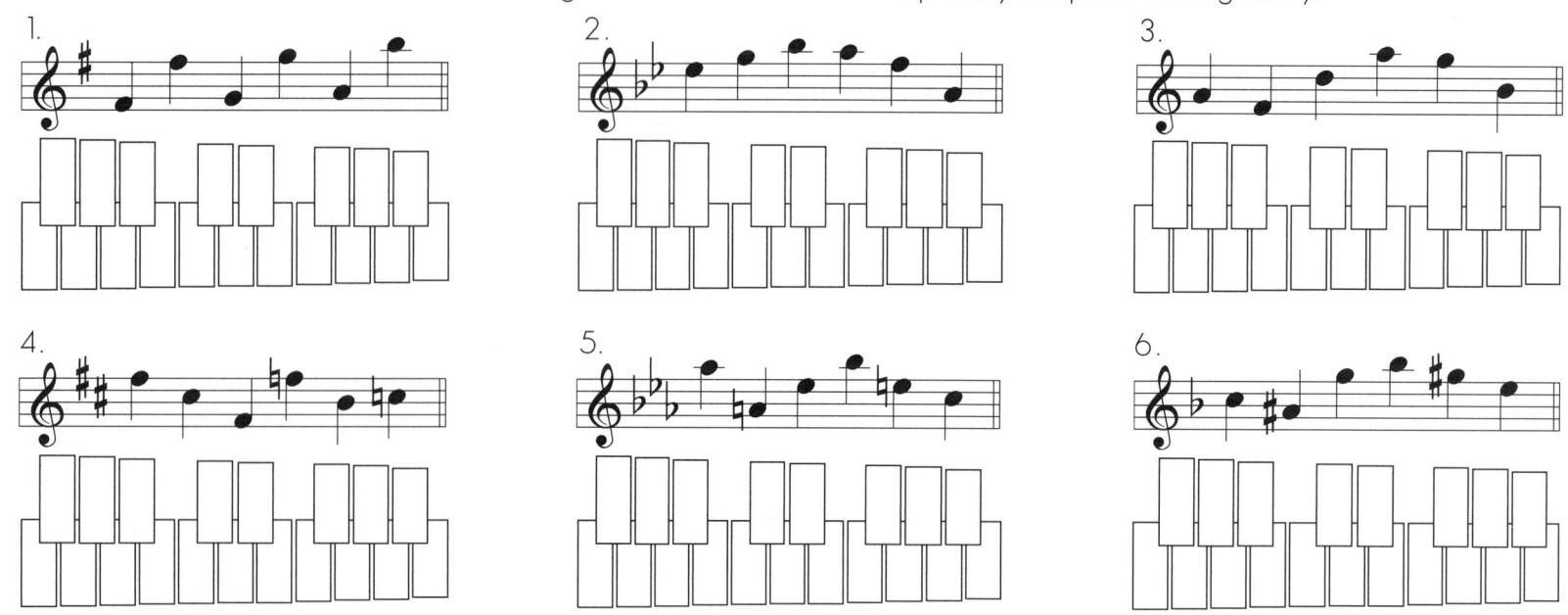

Speed Test #2: These easy lines are written in BASS CLEF. Write the note names in the blanks provided.

1. __ __ __ __
2. __ __ __ __
3. __ __ __ __
4. __ __ __ __
5. __ __ __ __
6. __ __ __ __
7. __ __ __ __
8. __ __ __ __

Music Reading Exercise: Work up each line separately before playing all four lines together.

64

Music Reading Exercises:
Finger through each line, saying the note names BEFORE you attempt to play!

Appendix: Lesson Thirteen

Speed Test #1: Find these notes in BASS CLEF, then write the note name on the correct key on the keyboard.

Duet for two players

①

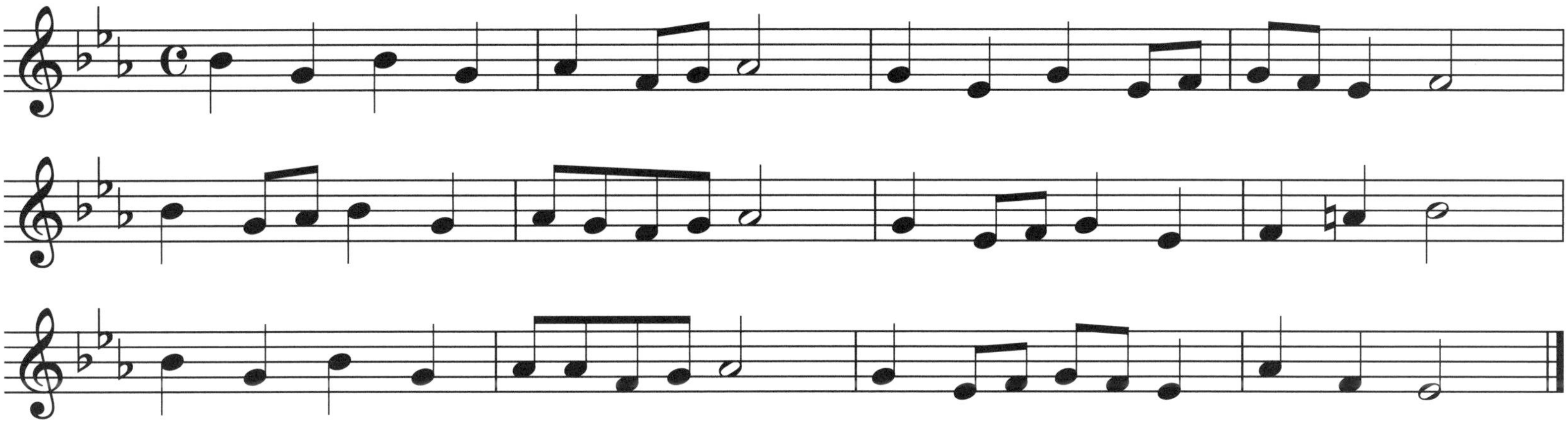

②

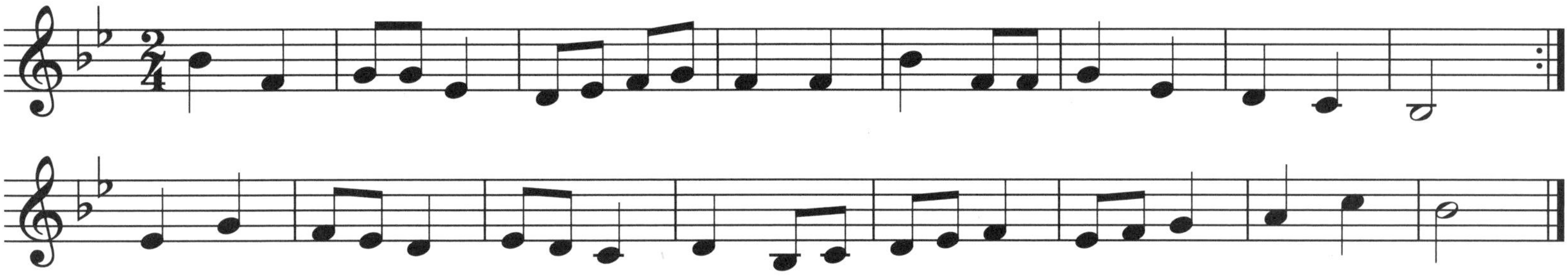

③

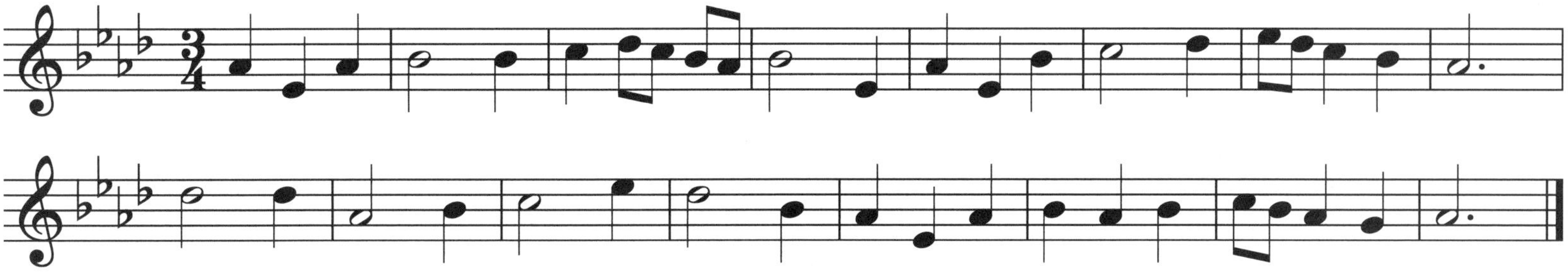

④

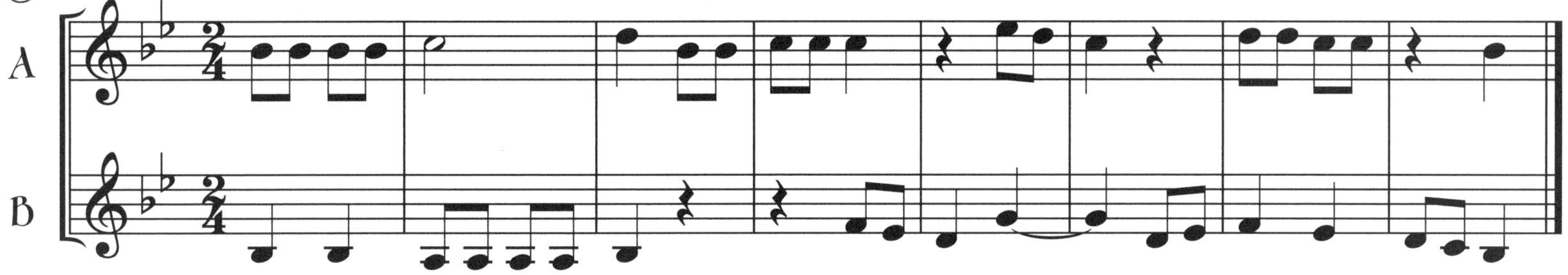

⑤

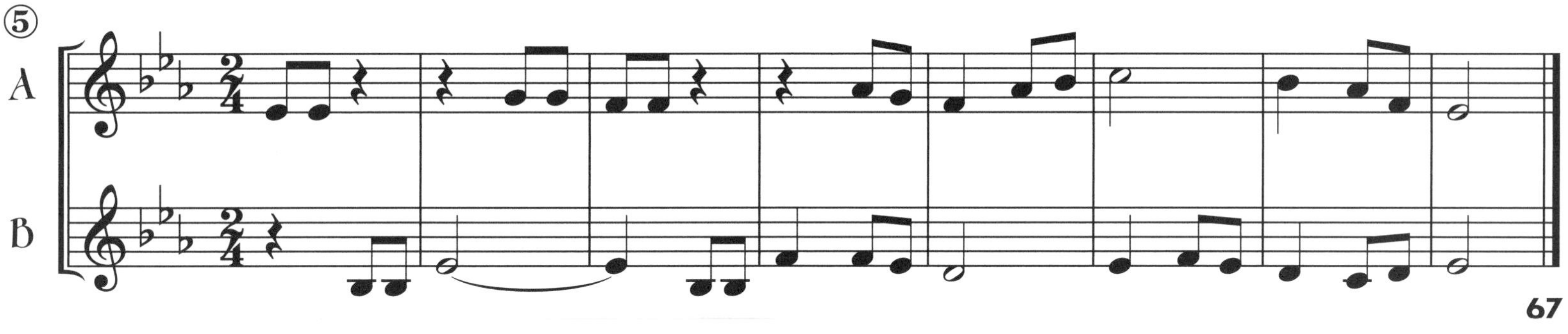

Appendix: Lesson Fourteen

Speed Test #2: These lines are written in BASS CLEF. You know the routine.

Duet for two players

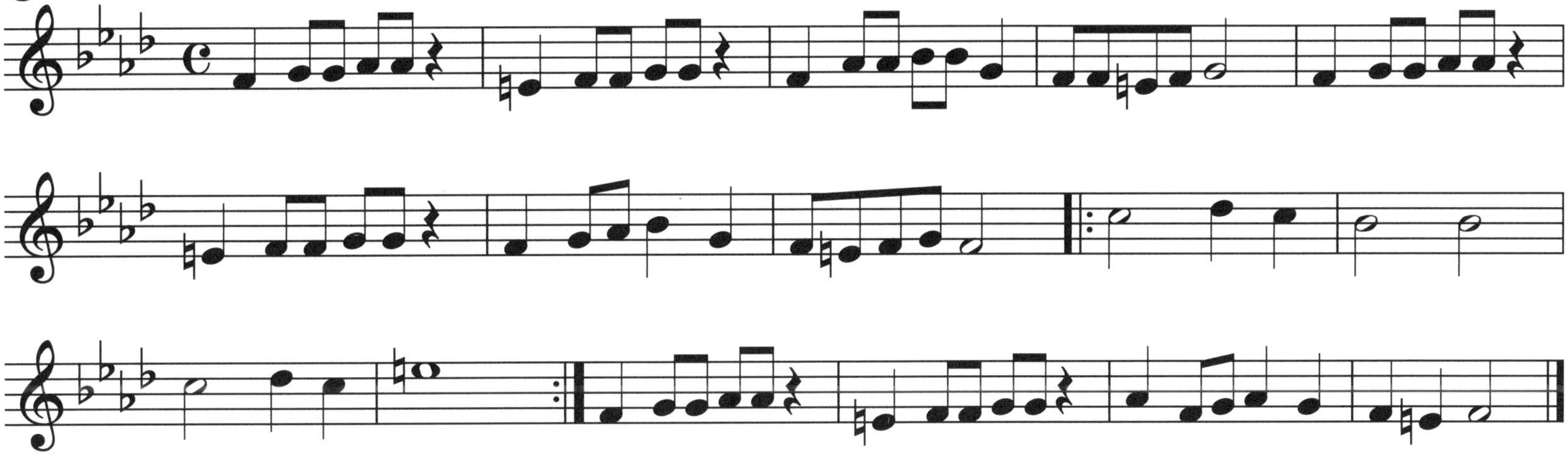

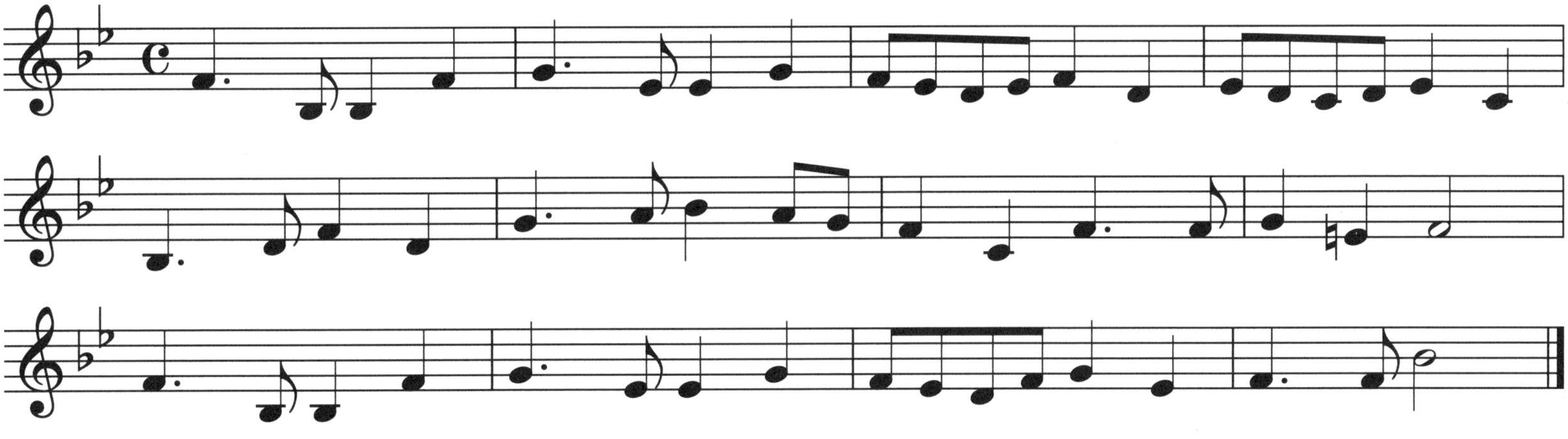

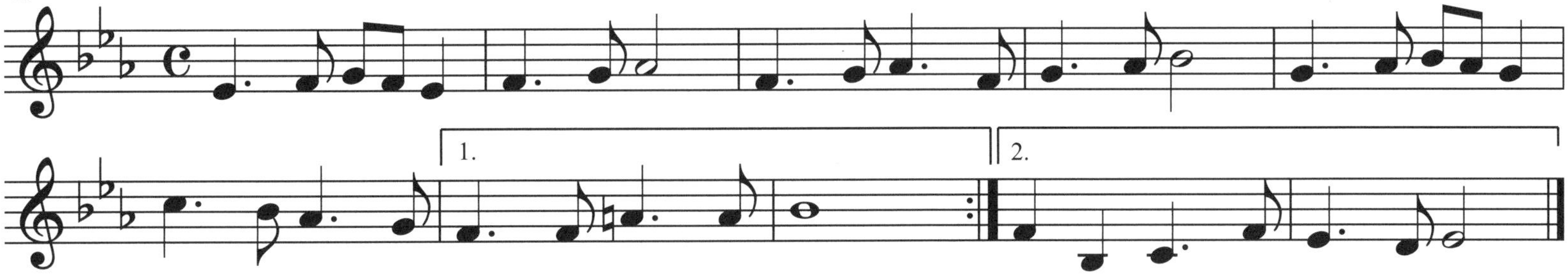

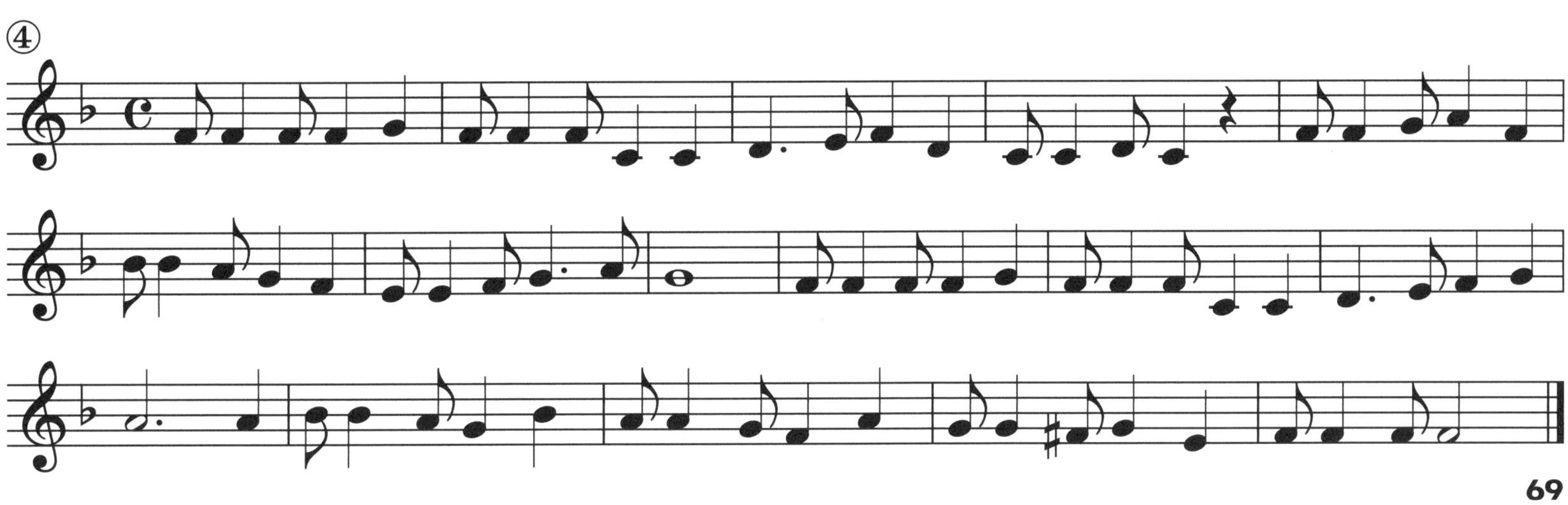

Appendix: Lesson Fifteen

Speed Test #1: Draw these notes ON the **treble** staff (no ledger lines!) using as many different types of NOTE VALUES that you can think of (so far, you've had seven different types in your music)!

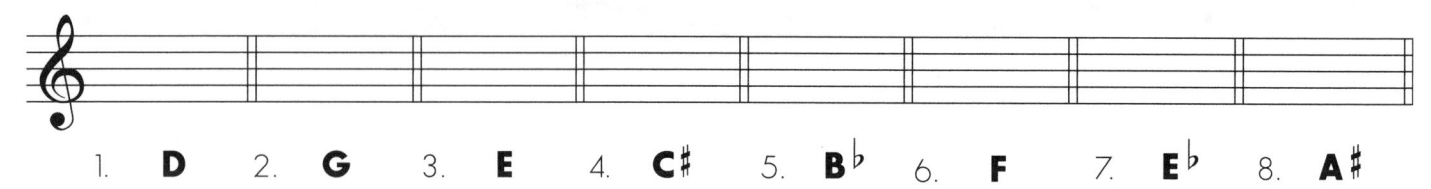

1. **D**   2. **G**   3. **E**   4. **C♯**   5. **B♭**   6. **F**   7. **E♭**   8. **A♯**

Speed Test #2: Same rules, this time in **bass clef**. Remember that stem direction is very important!

1. **D**   2. **G**   3. **E**   4. **C♯**   5. **B♭**   6. **F**   7. **E♭**   8. **A♯**

Music Reading Exercises

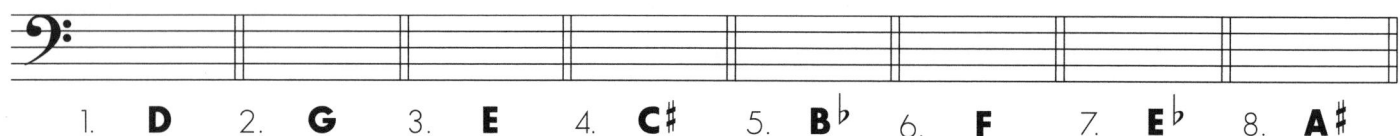

Duet

Appendix: Lesson Sixteen

Speed Test #1: Match the musical term with the correct definition by putting the letter in the blank.

1. _____ **Moderato**
2. _____ **Crescendo**
3. _____ **Time Signature**
4. _____ f
5. _____ **Diminuendo**
6. _____ **Largo**
7. _____ **Double Bar Line**
8. _____ ♯
9. _____ **Allegro**
10. _____ **Bar Line**
11. _____ **Tie**
12. _____ **Andante**
13. _____ p
14. _____ **Tempo**
15. _____ ♭
16. _____ **Presto**
17. _____ **Key Signature**
18. _____ mf
19. _____ **Accelerando**
20. _____ **Ledger Lines**

A Play in a FAST tempo
B Play SOFT
C To gradually play FASTER
D To gradually play LOUDER
E RAISES the pitch of a note one half step
F Play in a VERY FAST tempo
G Play LOUD
H Tells you which notes to play flat or sharp though the piece
I Play in a MEDIUM tempo
J To gradually play SOFTER
K Lines used to extend the range of the staff
L Describes the SPEED of the music
M Tells you when you've reached the end of the song
N A line that connects two notes together
O To play MEDIUM volume
P Tells you how many beats in a measure
Q Play in a VERY SLOW tempo
R LOWERS the pitch of a note one half step
S Play in a SLOW tempo
T Separates notes into measures

Music Reading Exercises: Try to see each "pattern" in these exercises. Read each <u>pattern</u> instead of individual notes!

Appendix: Lesson Seventeen

Speed Test #1: Check the CLEF before beginning each of these lines!

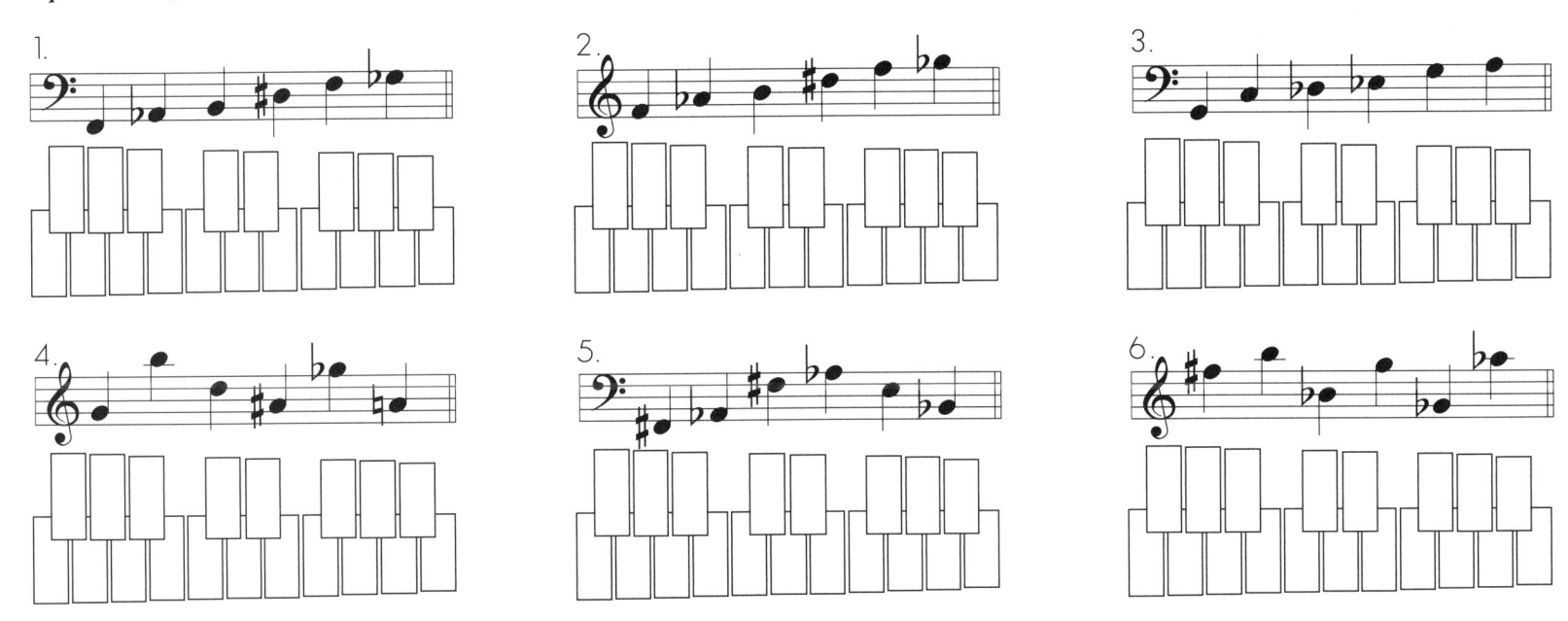

Speed Test #2: Draw a whole note on the correct **interval** (up or down) from the starting pitch given.

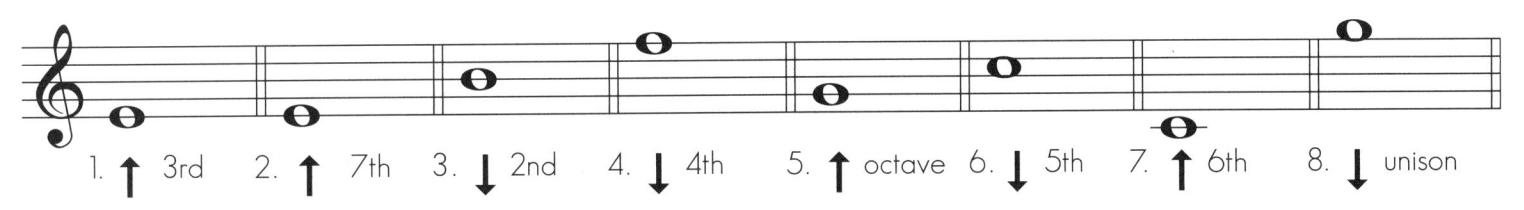

1. ↑ 3rd   2. ↑ 7th   3. ↓ 2nd   4. ↓ 4th   5. ↑ octave   6. ↓ 5th   7. ↑ 6th   8. ↓ unison

Music Reading Exercises:
These lines again are based on patterns. Find the pattern before you attempt to read.

①

②

73

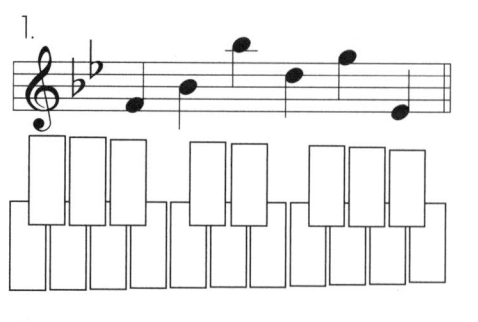

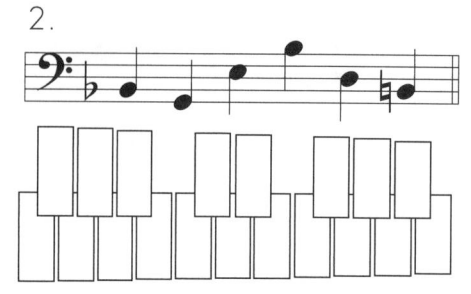

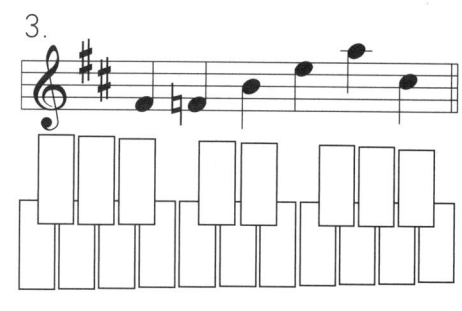

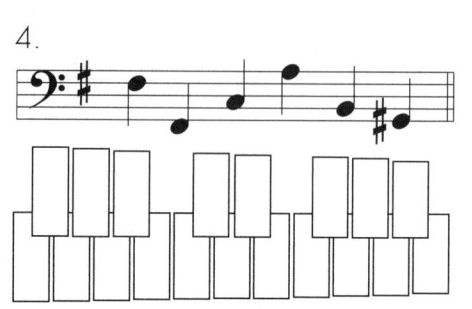

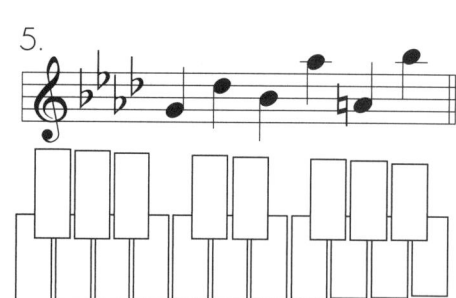

Appendix: Lesson Eighteen

Speed Test #1: Check the clef AND the key signature on each of these lines!

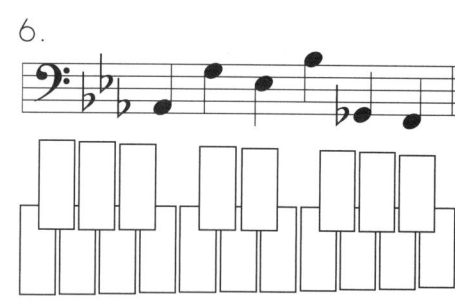

Music Reading Exercises:

Speed Test #2:   Name the interval between the two notes.

1. _____ 2. _____ 3. _____ 4. _____ 5. _____ 6. _____ 7. _____ 8. _____ 9. _____ 10. _____

Music Reading Exercises:

④

⑤

⑥

Appendix: Lesson Nineteen

Speed Test #1: Given the starting pitch, build the MAJOR SCALES by writing the correct note name on the keys.

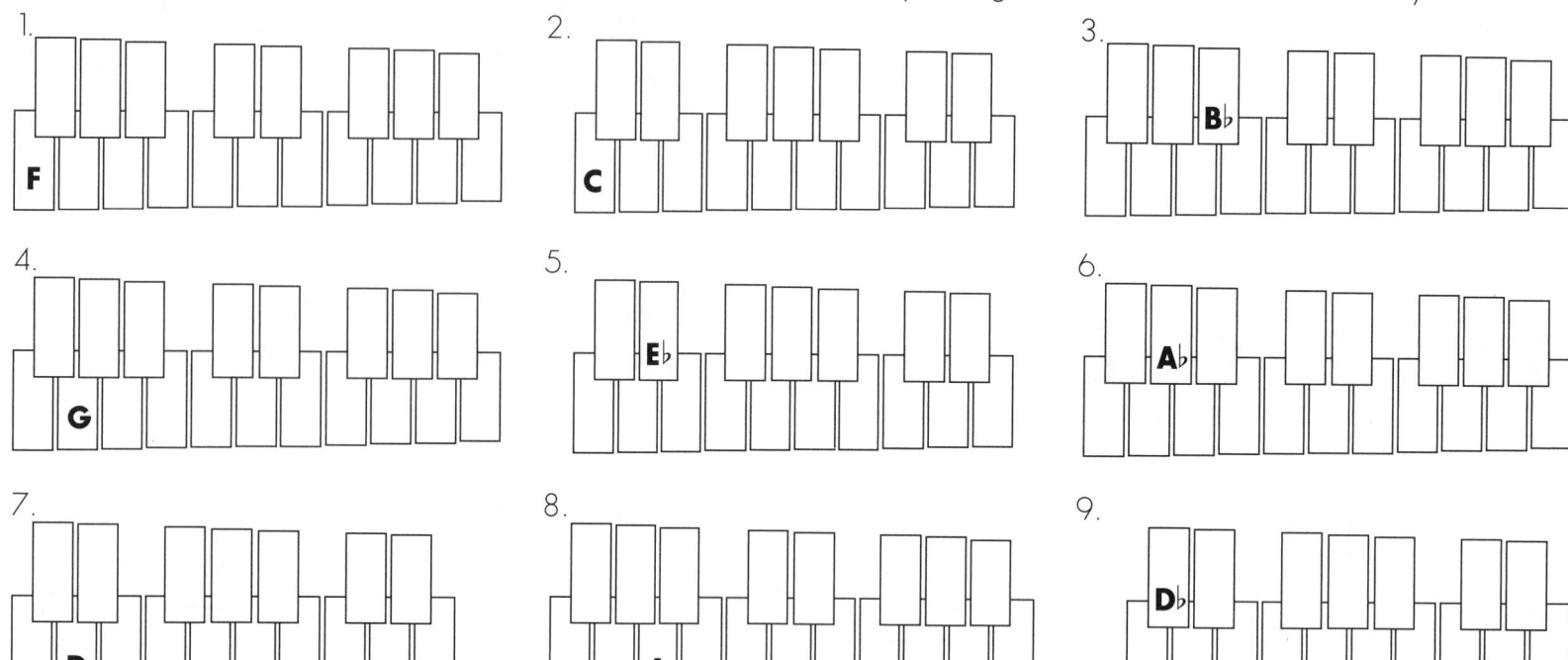

1. F
2. C
3. B♭
4. G
5. E♭
6. A♭
7. D
8. A
9. D♭

Music Reading Exercises:

Speed Test #2:   Watch the key signature when finding these pitches in bass clef.

Music Reading Exercises:

Appendix: Lesson Twenty

Speed Test #1: Finally! The last "find the note" speed test! In addition to these exercises, you should have passed off all ten levels of the SPEED NOTE READING TUTOR at the "pro" level!

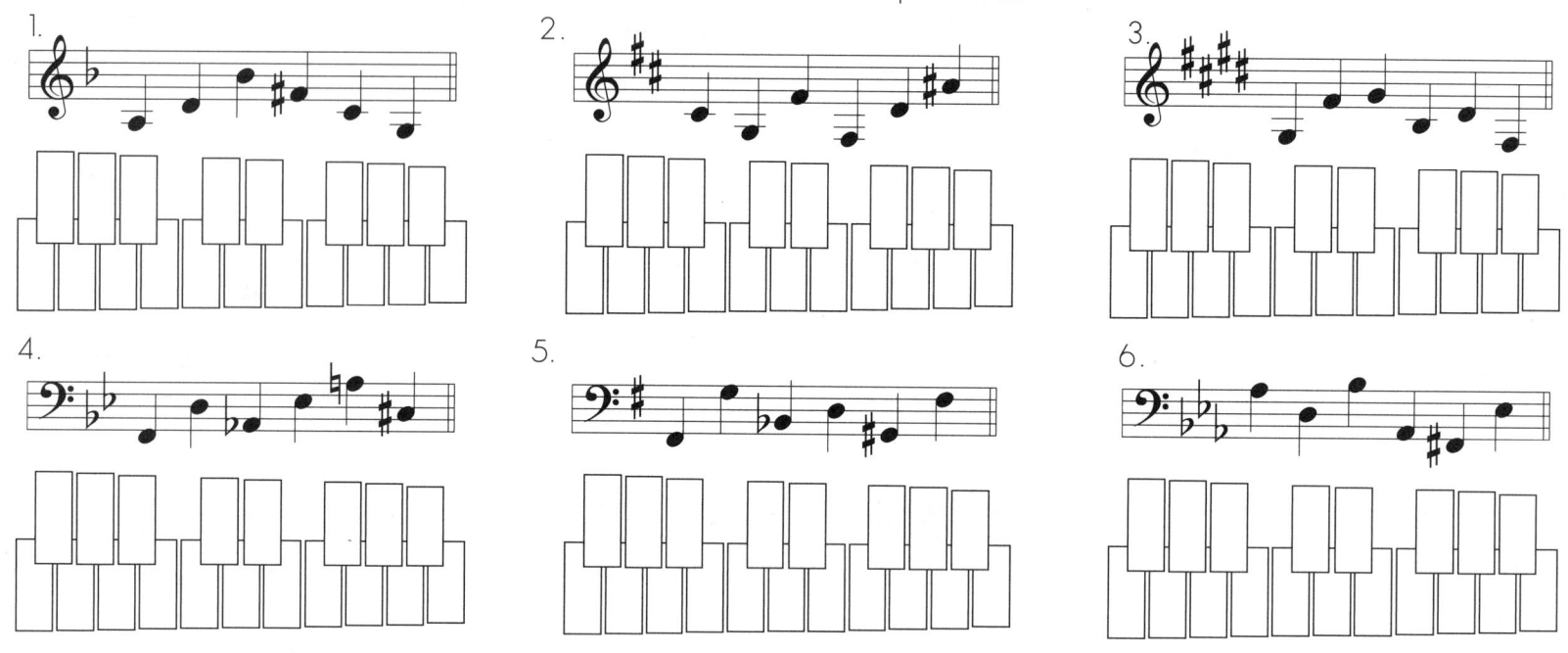

Music Reading Exercises:

Duet for two players

An Introduction to the Timpani

The word "**timpani**" is taken from the Latin word "timpanum," meaning "vibrating membrane." The timpani's heads, when struck, are made to vibrate. The timpani are often called kettle drums because the bowls, which are made from copper, resemble kettles. Timpan_i_ is the Italian plural, timpano is singular (although you'll almost always hear someone refer to a single drum as timpani or just "timp"). A percussionist who plays the timpani is sometimes referred to as the "timpanist."

Timpani range in size from 32 inches to 23 inches (the standard sizes are 32", 29", 26", and 23" – 3 inches for each separate size).

Unlike most drums in the percussion family, timpani produce a definite pitch when struck. The timpani are tuned to specific pitches by using pedals which, by use of a mechanism, stretch the heads across the rim of the bowl. Because of its low pitch, music for timpani is written in the BASS CLEF.

SPECIAL BONUS!
VIDEO LESSONS OF ALL THE TECHNIQUES AND EXERCISES ARE AVAILABLE ON YOUTUBE! Search for "Fresh Approach to Timpani" to find these helpful videos.

The Proper Beating Area

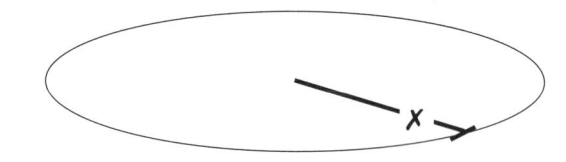

The proper beating spot on the timpani is approximately one-third the distance between the rim and the center of the head (about 3-4 inches from the rim). Since a timpano is a bowl, you do not strike it in the center as you do other types of percussion instruments. Because the bowl acts as a resonating chamber, the sound vibrations have nowhere to travel when you hit the drum in the center.

Experiment playing on different areas of the drum until you find the best sound. Like the "sweet spot" on a bat or tennis racket, each timpani has a beating area that produces the best sound.

Hand Position

Grasp the timpani mallet just as you do a keyboard mallet. Instead of playing with "flat" hands, turn your wrists to where the thumb nail is facing the ceiling (this is known as the "French Style" of playing). Relax the back fingers – they should lightly make contact with the shaft of the mallet. For a darker, heavier tone, add more finger contact.

The Stroke Style

The "Prep Stroke"

Start with the stick about 3 inches from the head (with the "French" hand position)

Raise the forearm slightly while leaving the mallet head in the same position (causing the wrist to rotate as if you were shaking someone's hand).

As you continue to raise the forearm, allow the wrist to "react" to the motion.

The "Stroke"

Allow the weight of the forearm to carry the stick back to the timpani head. Again, the wrist (which is totally relaxed) should react to the movement of the arm – much like the way a baby's head would react when he or she is picked up suddenly by a mother.

The "Follow Through"

At the exact moment of impact of the mallet with the drum head, snap the wrist slightly - the way you would "pop" someone with a wet towel, or cast a fishing rod.

Allow the hand to come up to shoulder level, then gently bring the stick back to playing position. This is the most important part of the stroke because it "draws" the sound out of the instrument.

Practice the Stroke

Don't worry about tuning the drums yet – have your instructor tune these pitches for you. Each "prep stroke" in this exercise should begin one count before the note, and the "follow through" should last approximately one-half of the note's duration. Memorize this line so that you can watch your hands and the mallet placement on the timpani head.

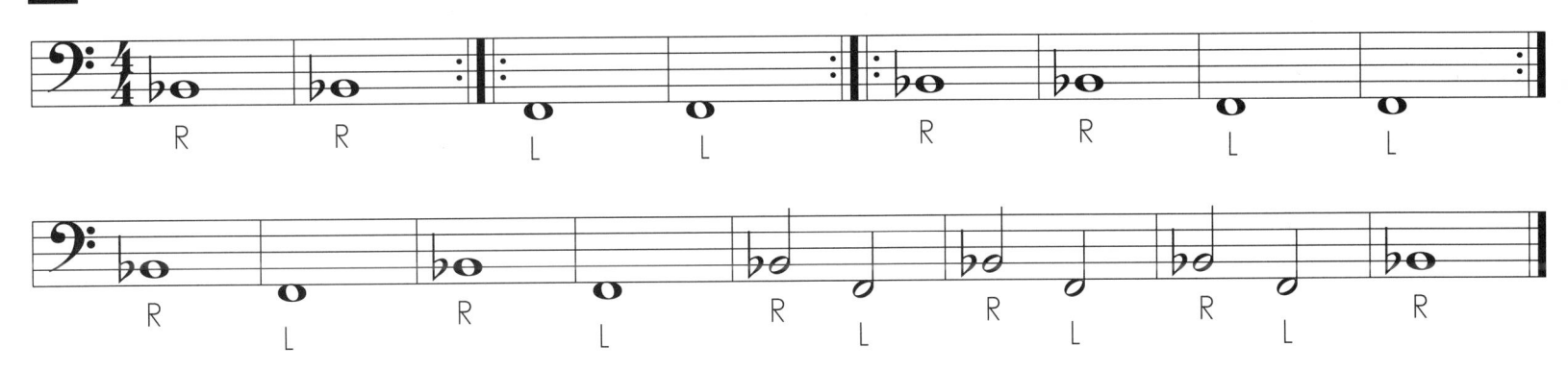

1 m.m. = 120

2 As you make the strokes on the drums on the first line in this exercise, rotate your upper body at the waist so that your hands remain centered on the drum. Try to make the prep strokes and follow throughs feel natural and relaxed.

3 Use the suggested sticking and alternate every stroke. Remember to follow through on each half note!

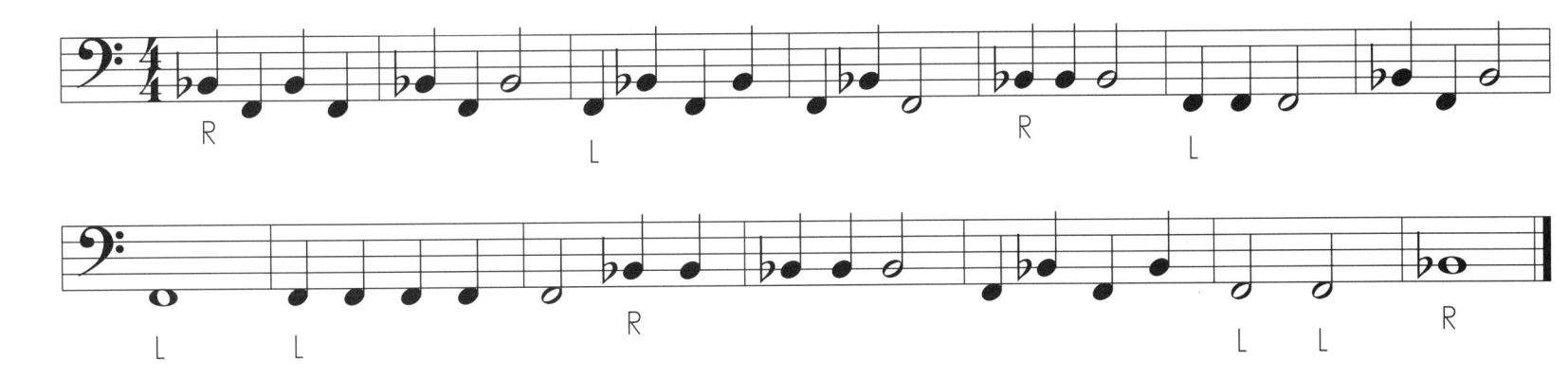

Tuning the Timpani

The first and most obvious step to tuning the timpani is to know what size timpani will reach the desired pitch. Spend some time memorizing these pitch ranges:

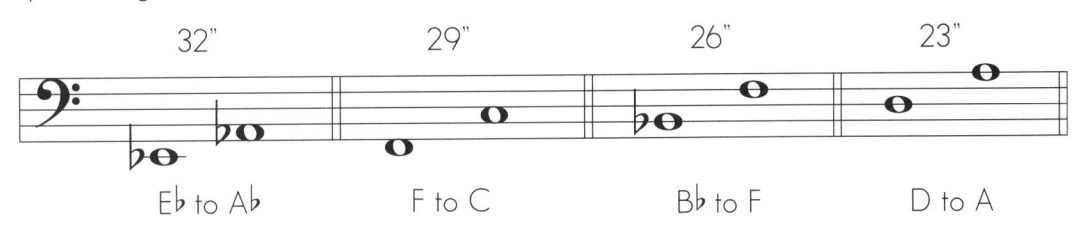

32" — Eb to Ab
29" — F to C
26" — Bb to F
23" — D to A

81

Tuning the Timpani, continued: Hearing and Singing the Pitch

The biggest problem that most percussionists have with tuning the timpani is being able to HEAR and SING the pitch! Start with a pitch pipe and see if you can sing or hum various pitches. You don't have to have a great singing voice to sing a pitch, but you will have to put some effort into it. If you can't sing a pitch, you won't be able to tell if the timpani are in tune!

My Easy, Never Fail (but not too sophisticated) Approach to Tuning

I have found that the easiest method of getting my students to hear the pitch on a timpano is to approach it like a bad country western singer. Start by playing a set of 2 pitches on a piano. Sing (or hum) the lowest note, then "scoop" up to the second.

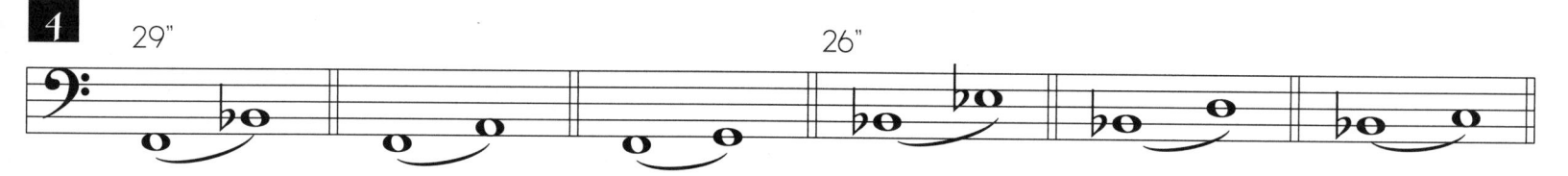

4 29"   26"

Now play the exercise above on the timpani. With the pedal at the bottom range of the timpani, strike the drum softly. Push the pedal up gradually until you hear the desired pitch. If you can work the pedal smoothly and slowly, you should be able to hear the same "scooping pitch" that you did when you sang.

SING THE PITCH INTO THE DRUM. Bend down close to the beating area and sing or hum the pitch into the timpani. If the drum is in tune with the pitch you are singing, the head will begin to vibrate (or, the drum will "sing back" to you). Listen to the vibrations to make slight adjustments up or down on the pedal to match the pitch perfectly.

Decide which drums you should use to tune these following notes, then give it your best shot.

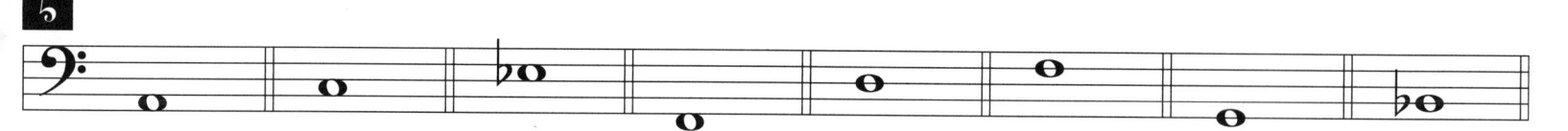

5

DIRECTORS: avoid telling the students "A little higher" or "A little lower!" If the student misses the pitch, start over from scratch!

Passing Strokes

It is often necessary for the sticks to pass from one drum to another without the luxury of having a half note or rest to give you time for a smooth transition. To produce the best possible sound on each drum, it is necessary to eliminate as many "cross stickings" as possible. Consider this example:

If you start the 8th notes on the RIGHT hand, it is necessary for the right stick to <u>cross</u> the left on the passing

R L R L R   R L R L R

Of course, the simple solution would be to start the 8th notes on the LEFT hand to avoid the cross over stroke.

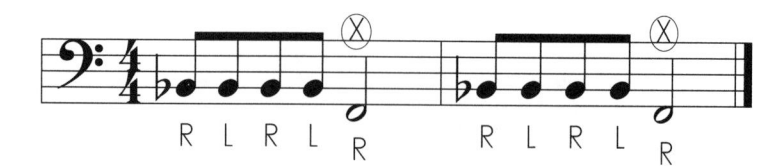

L R L R L   L R L R L

To develop the proper sticking for passing strokes, you must first decide if the group of notes directly before the passing stroke is "EVEN" or "ODD." Odd groups of notes should start with the <u>outside</u> mallet (the mallet that's the greatest distance from the drum that you are passing <u>to</u>). Even groups of notes should start with the <u>inside</u> mallet. Proper sticking habits must be "second nature" to a timpanist! Work on the next exercises for a few weeks with a metronome set on 120.

82

Passing from the high drum to the low drum:

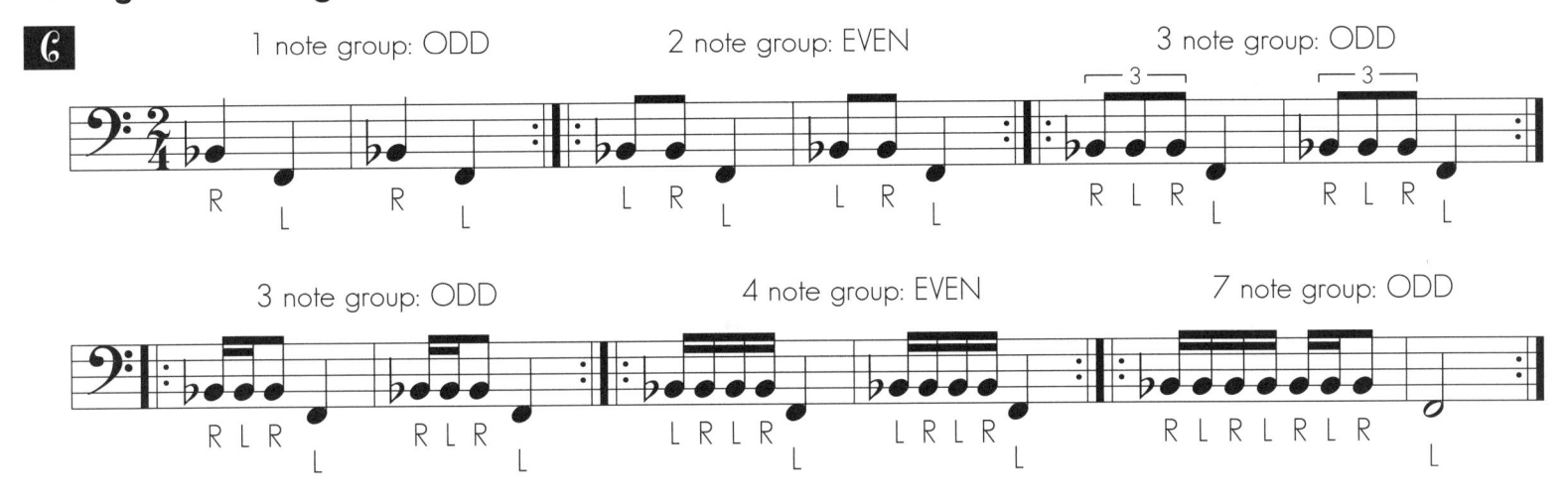

Passing from low to high:

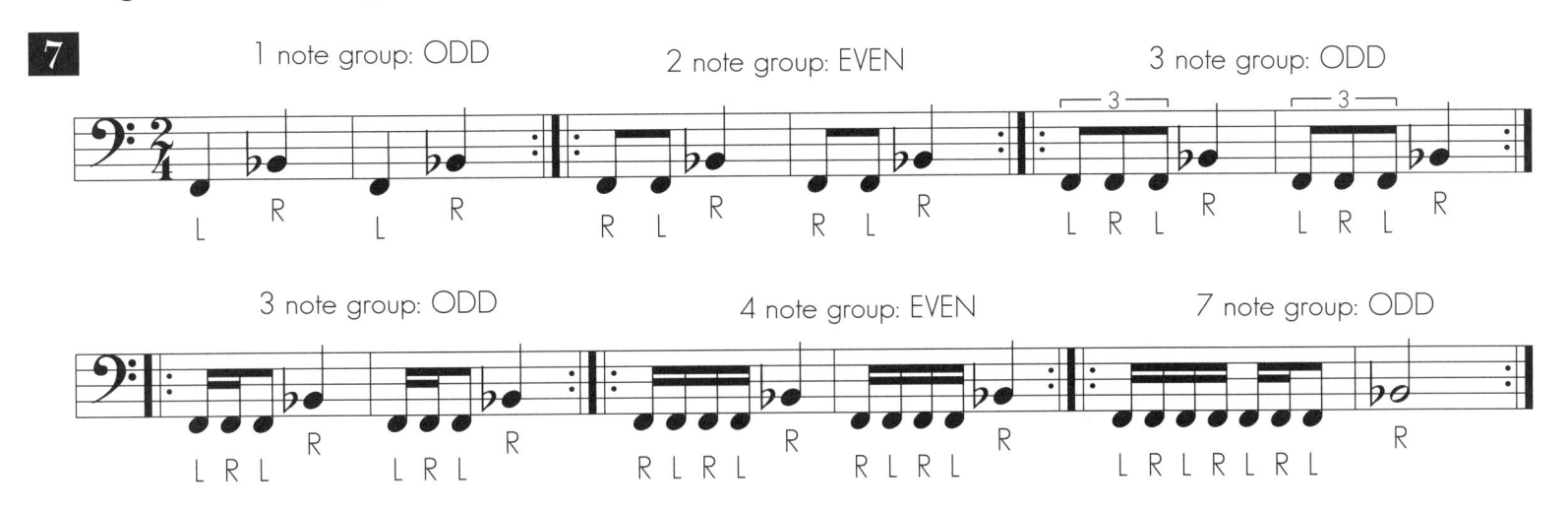

Muffling the Timpani

You can control the vibration of the timpani head by the use of muffling. Hold the mallet with the thumb and index finger, then place the back three fingers gently on the head near the beating area. Try to muffle the drum as quietly as possible! Avoid slapping the drum or creating any unwanted sounds.

Practice muffling the drum on the rests in this exercise. Each note should be given its exact value, and no sound should occur in the rests. Start with a very slow tempo (quarter = 80), then speed up as you get more accustomed to muffling techniques.

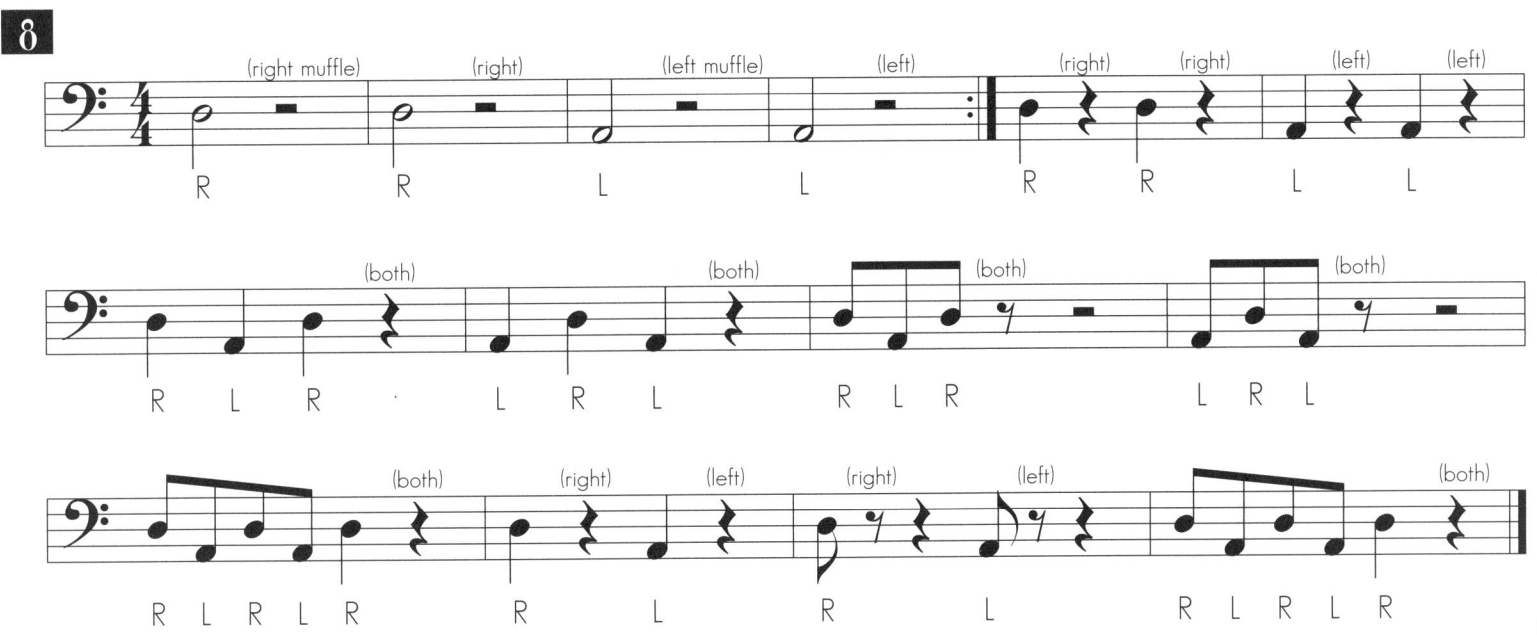

Playing Rolls on the Timpani

The purpose of the roll on timpani is to sustain an even sounding tone. A wind player does this by blowing air through the instrument, a string player does it by drawing the bow across the string. Since the sound of the timpani note decays as soon as it is hit with the mallet, we must sustain a tone by rapidly striking the drum. To accomplish this, relax the wrists as much as possible and play with quick, EVEN strokes single strokes (never play bounce rolls on the timpani).

11

You may notice that it is easier to produce a nice sounding roll on the lower drum. That is because a loose timpani head has a slower VIBRATION speed than a tight head. In order to keep the head vibrating, you can play with a slower roll speed. Try tuning the smallest timpani to the highest pitch and see how fast you must roll to keep the vibrations going!

The Passing Roll

When playing a passing roll (or slur), it is necessary to pass from one drum to the other without a break in the roll. Just like in the passing stroke exercises, you must always shift to the next drum with the INSIDE mallet first, avoiding a cross stroke. Try this 16th note exercise first, then speed it up until the 16th notes become rolls.

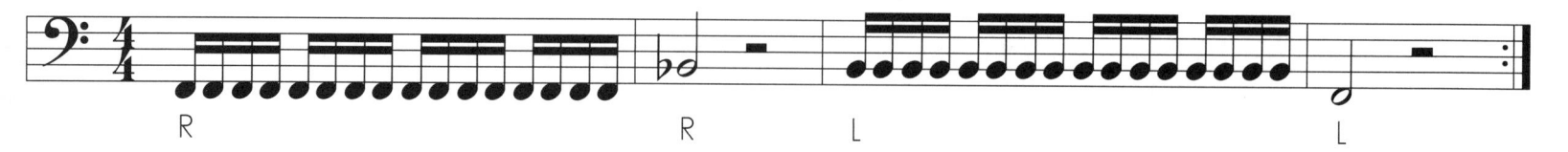

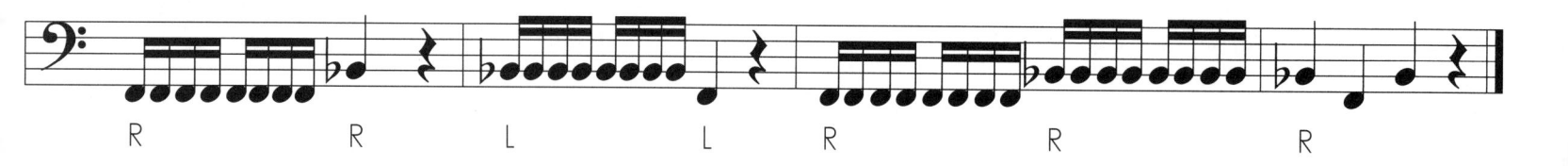

12

Of course, you may not be able to always play an even number of strokes on passing rolls. In this next exercise, try to move from one drum to the next as SMOOTHLY as possible, without any breaks in the sound.

13 *Adagio*

Timpani Etudes

Read the key signature when finding out which two notes to tune in this etude. Remember to stop all sound possible on each rest by muffling as quietly as possible. Follow the sticking when it's provided for you.

1 *Allegro*

This short etude includes some **staccato** notes (measure 15 and 16). When a dot is placed above or below a note, play the drum, then muffle as quickly as possible.

2 *March Tempo*

85

Accurate and silent muffling is extremely important in this slow etude. While all sound should stop on each rest, make sure that each note gets its full value.

3 *Adagio*

This etude includes a couple of quick tuning changes (meas. 12 and 20). Practice the tuning change several times to get used to the "foot action." While it might be easier to play this etude with 3 drums, GREAT TIMPANISTS will be able to play it on two!

4 *Moderato*

86

This etude is much more difficult and will take a few weeks to master. Have your teacher explain: **D.C. al Coda**, **sfp rolls**, and **Tempo I**. Try to play this etude with a feeling of one beat to the measure.

Technique Exercises: Alternating Stroke Studies

Work with a metronome as you practice these technique exercises to help you keep a steady tempo. Start slow, use full wrist strokes and strive to play each note in the correct beating spot. If you can play a line FOUR times without a single missed note, then speed the tempo up 10 beats. Transpose each exercise to each of the 12 major scales (take a different one each week).

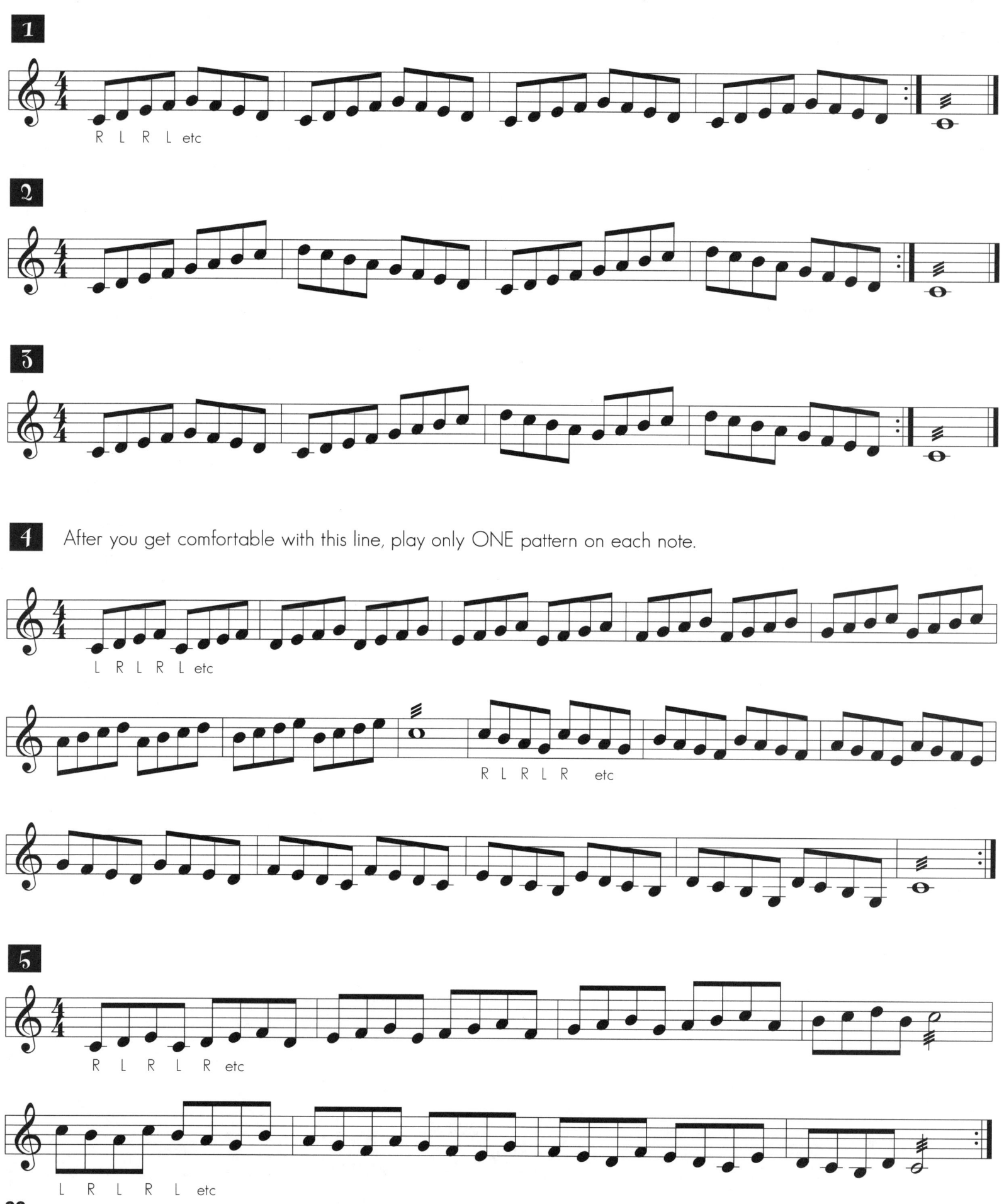

1

R L R L etc

2

3

4 After you get comfortable with this line, play only ONE pattern on each note.

L R L R L etc

R L R L R etc

5

R L R L R etc

L R L R L etc

9 This excerpt from "Flight of the Bumble Bee" is a little harder to learn, but makes a great chromatic scale exercise!

Technique Exercises: Rolls

While other instrumentalists may use air to sustain a pitch, percussionists must play rapid SINGLE strokes on the mallet instrument to sustain a sound (multiple bounce rolls do not work on the keyboard)! This exercise is an example of the **single stroke roll**. Start very slowly, then gradually speed up until you are playing fast single strokes, then gradually slow back to the original tempo. Practice this rudiment everyday to develop a smooth sounding roll!

1

Notice this exercise uses a "short-hand'" for 16th notes: quarter notes with two slashes. Practice this with a metronome and make sure that all of the 16th's are even (no breaks between the notes). Gradually speed up until the 16th notes become rolls.

2

3

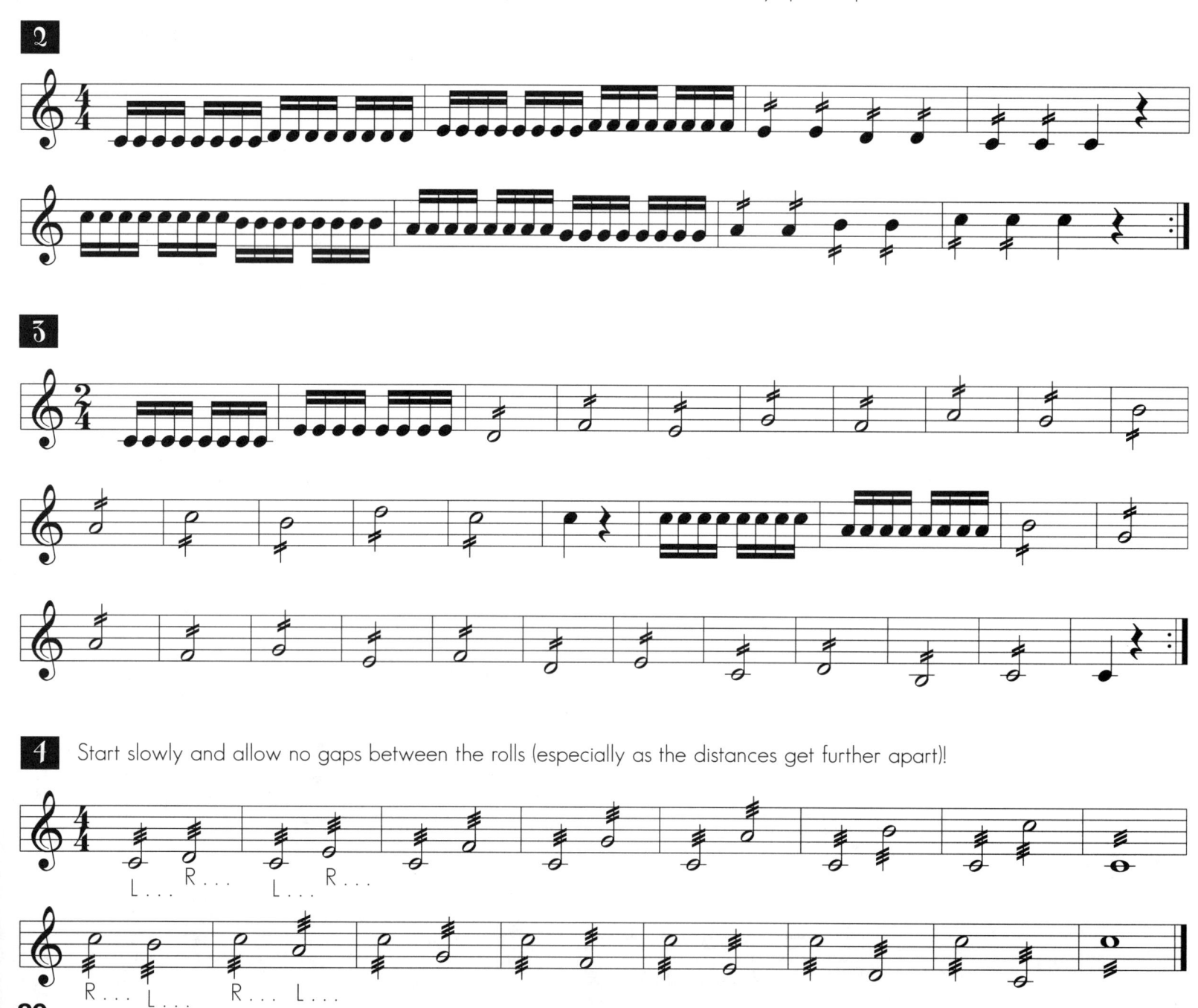

4 Start slowly and allow no gaps between the rolls (especially as the distances get further apart)!

L... R... L... R...

R... L... R... L...

90

Technique Exercises: Double Stops

As you play these double stop exercises, make sure that the two hands hit precisely together (no "flams")!

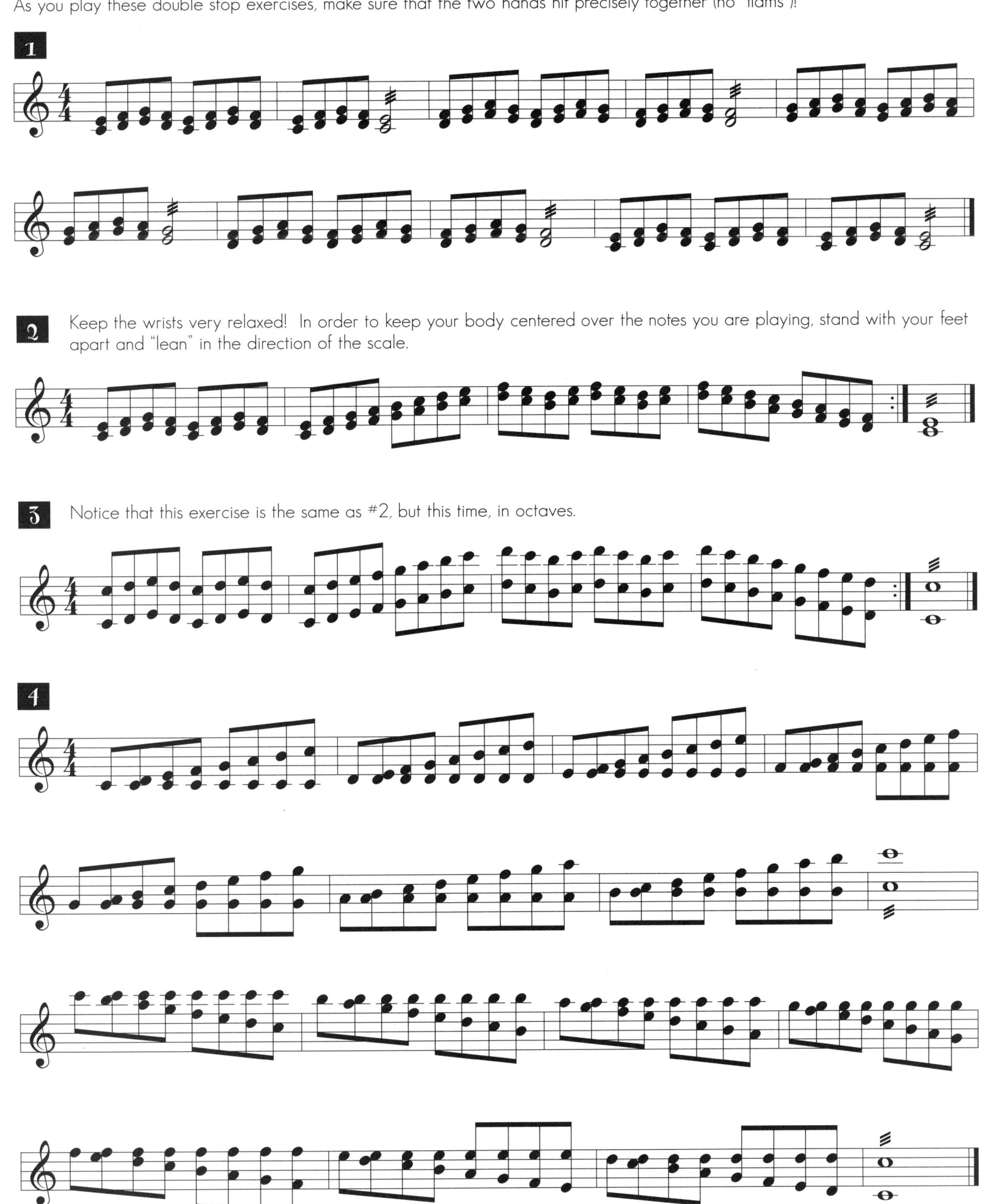

1

2 Keep the wrists very relaxed! In order to keep your body centered over the notes you are playing, stand with your feet apart and "lean" in the direction of the scale.

3 Notice that this exercise is the same as #2, but this time, in octaves.

4

Tetrachords / Major Scales

Major scales are built with two tetrachords connected by a whole step.

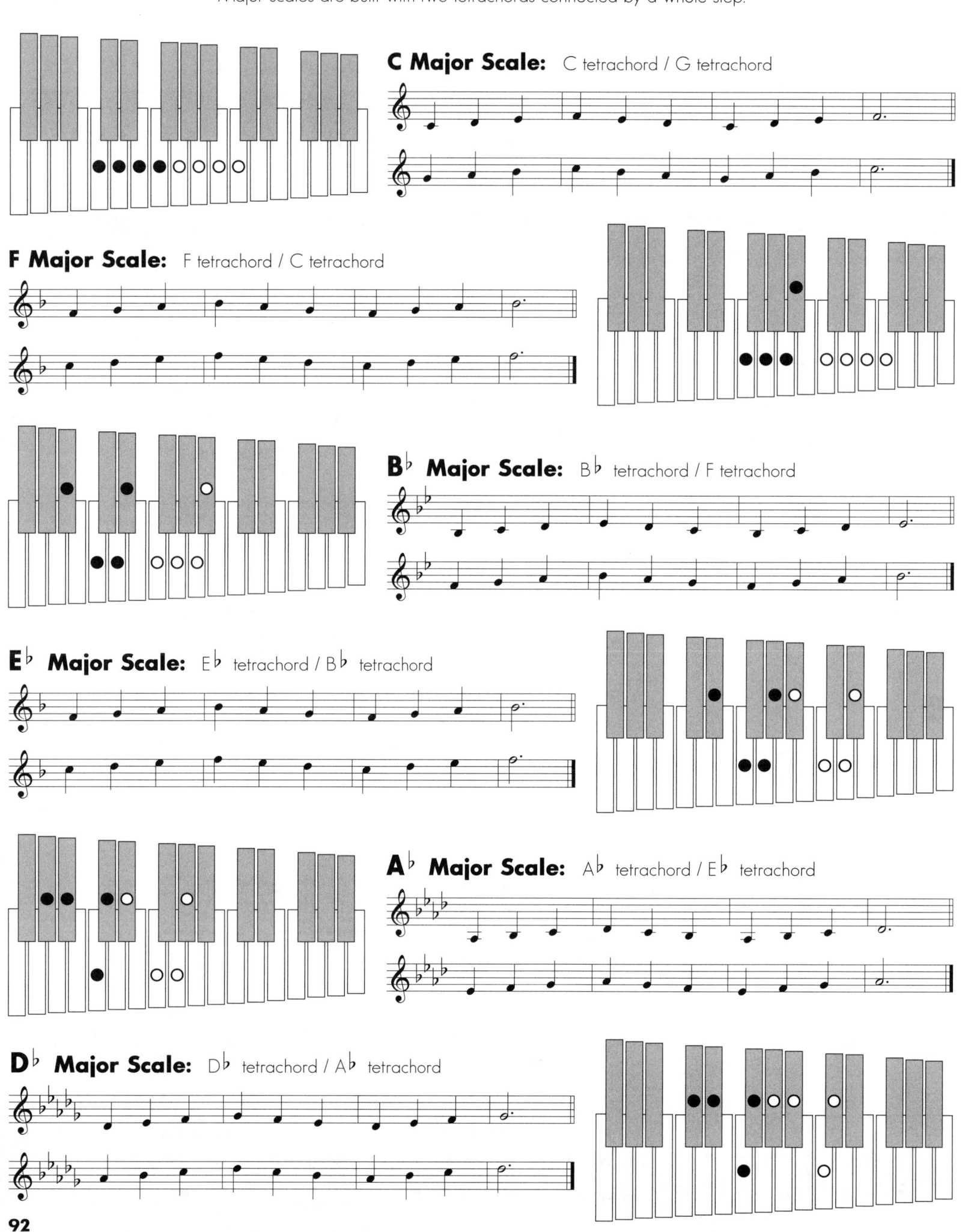

C Major Scale: C tetrachord / G tetrachord

F Major Scale: F tetrachord / C tetrachord

B♭ Major Scale: B♭ tetrachord / F tetrachord

E♭ Major Scale: E♭ tetrachord / B♭ tetrachord

A♭ Major Scale: A♭ tetrachord / E♭ tetrachord

D♭ Major Scale: D♭ tetrachord / A♭ tetrachord

G♭ Major Scale: G♭ tetrachord / D♭ tetrachord

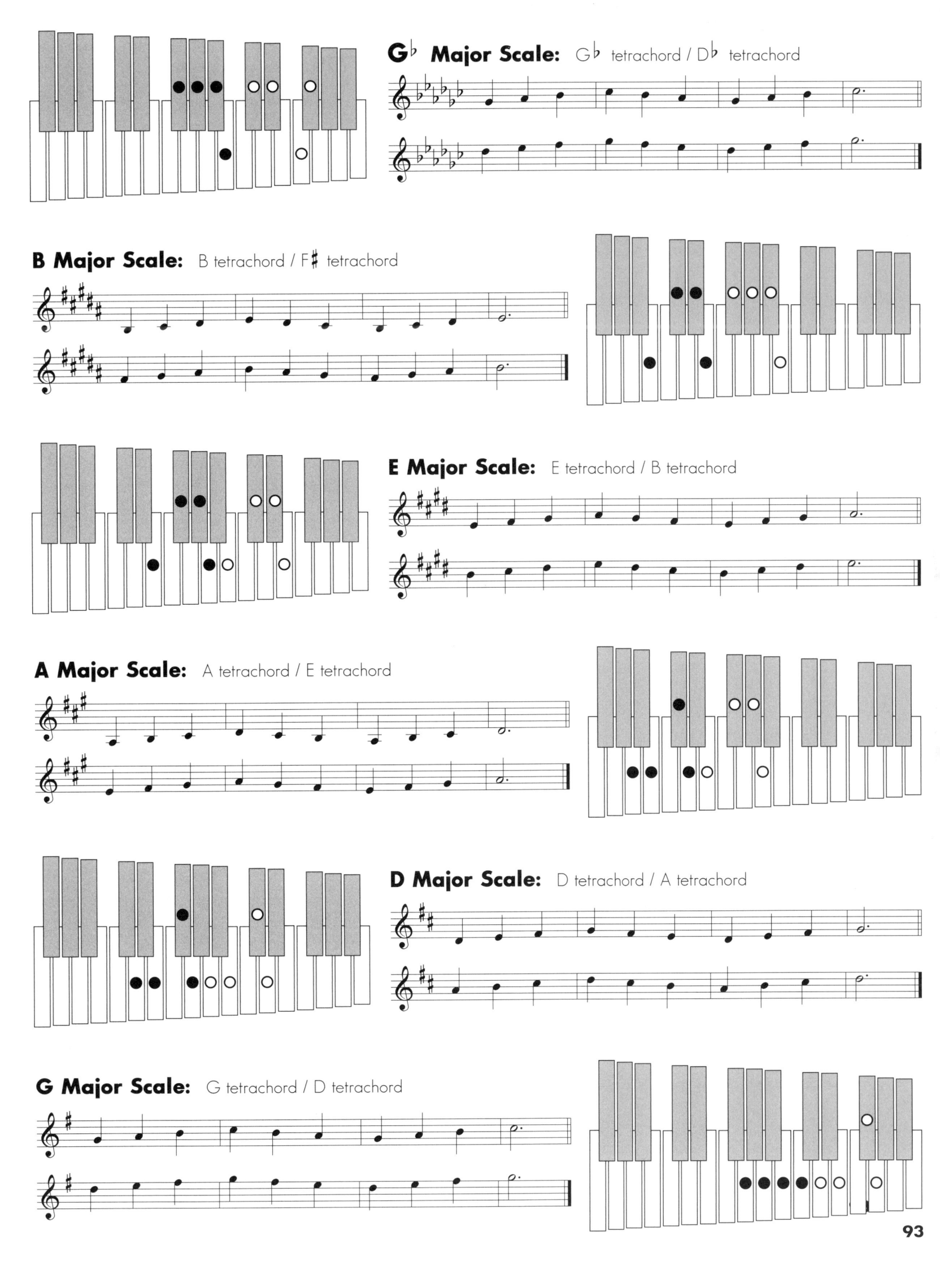

B Major Scale: B tetrachord / F# tetrachord

E Major Scale: E tetrachord / B tetrachord

A Major Scale: A tetrachord / E tetrachord

D Major Scale: D tetrachord / A tetrachord

G Major Scale: G tetrachord / D tetrachord

Major Scales & Arpeggios

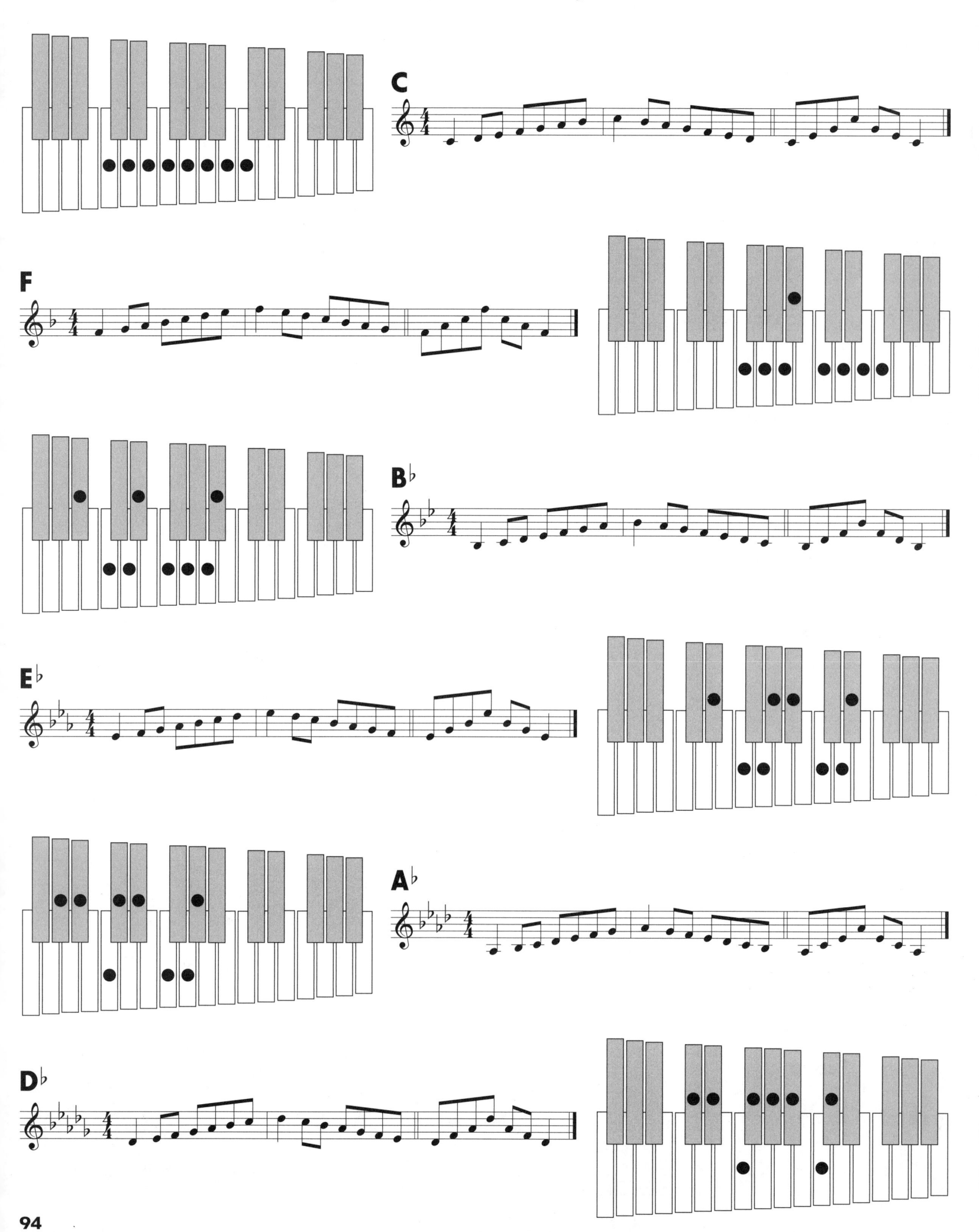

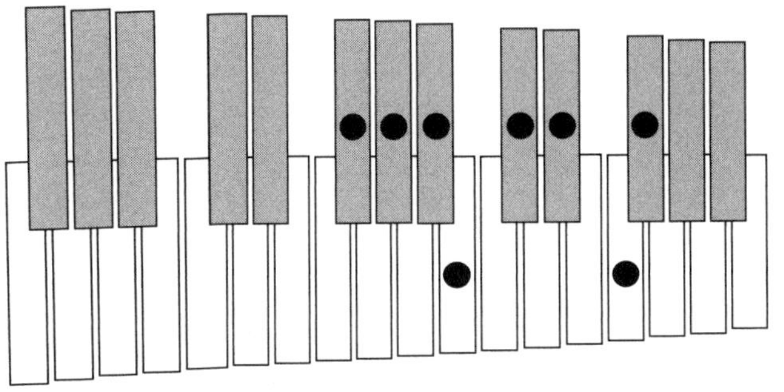

G♭

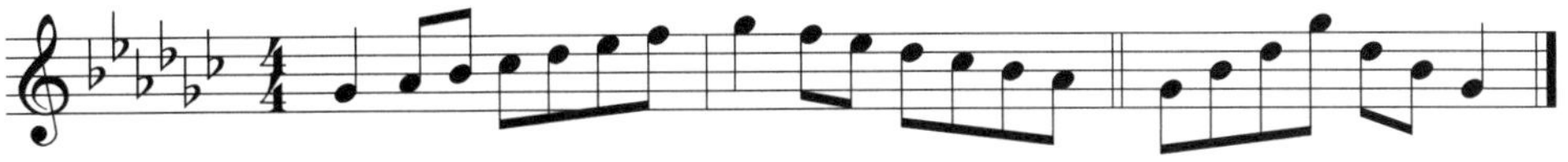

B

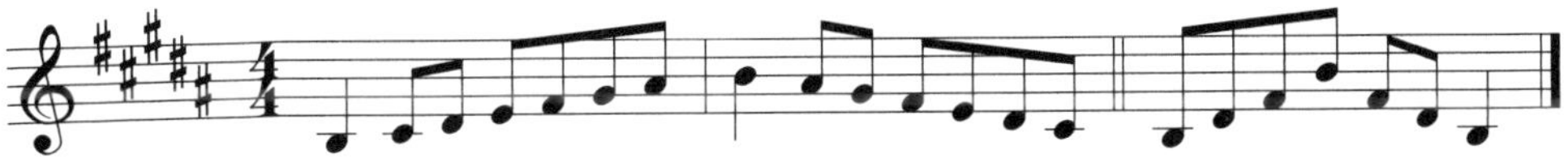

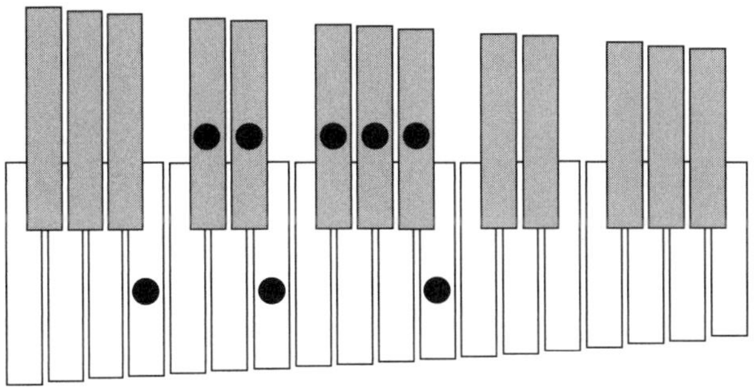

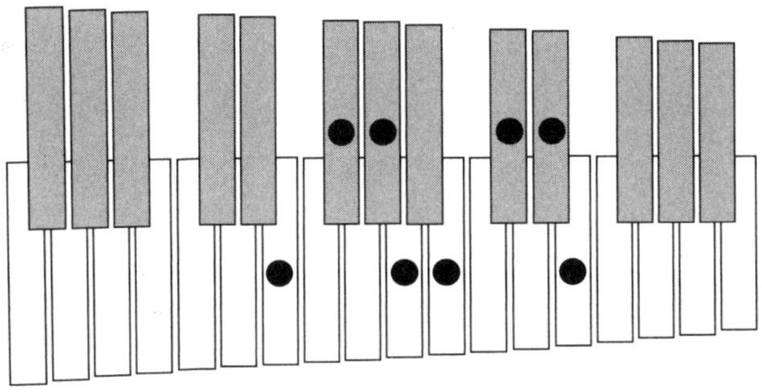

E

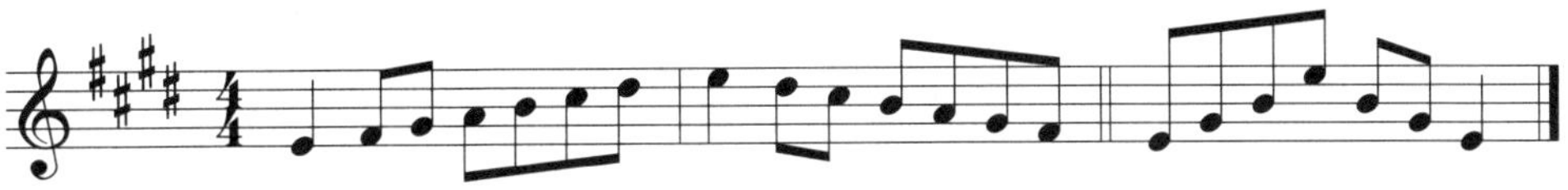

A

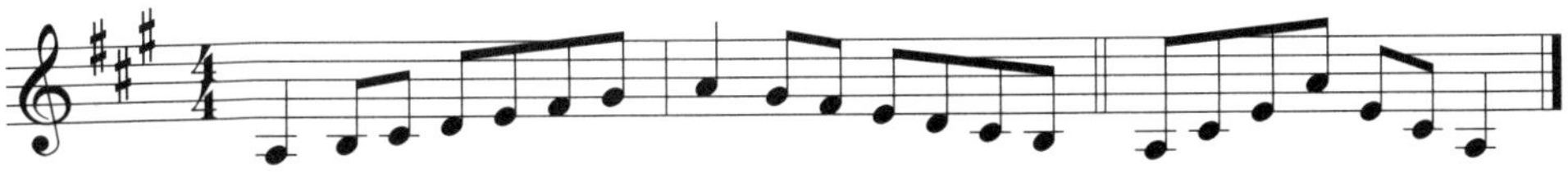

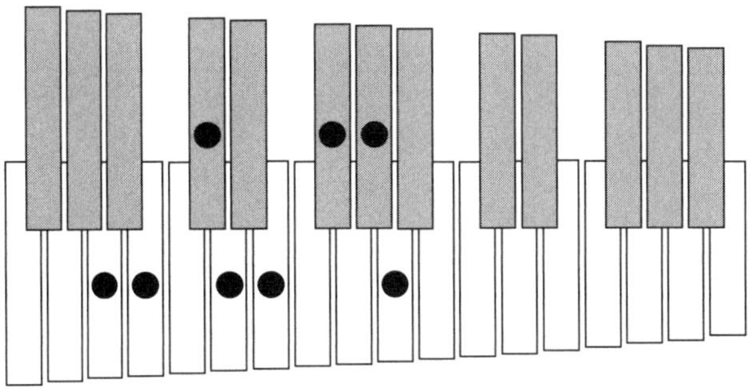

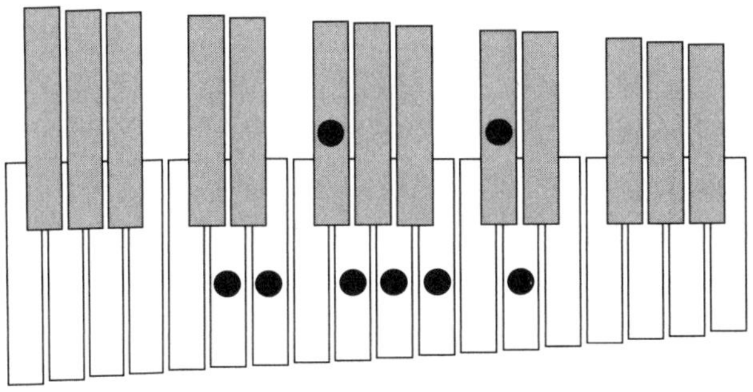

D

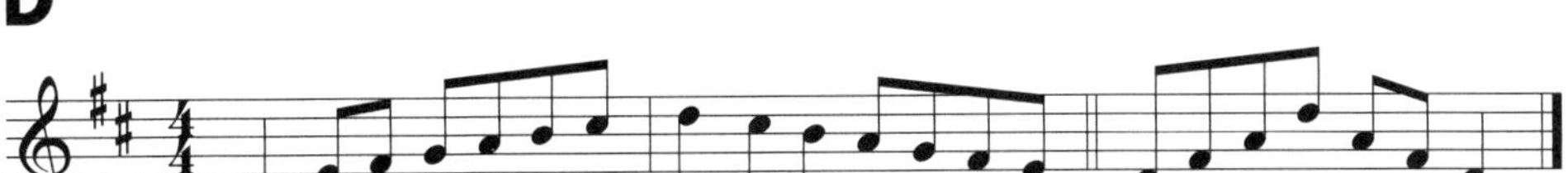

G

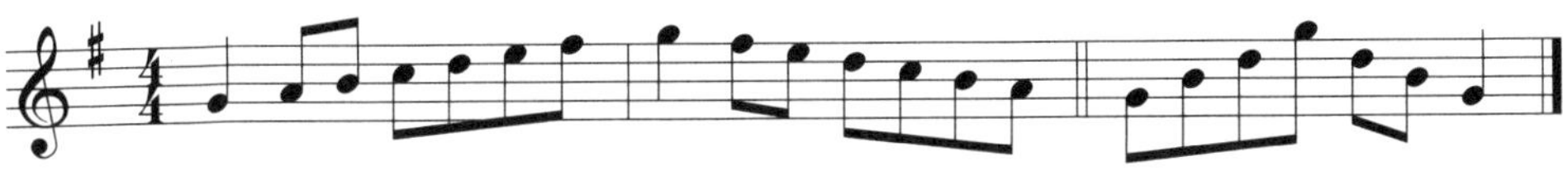

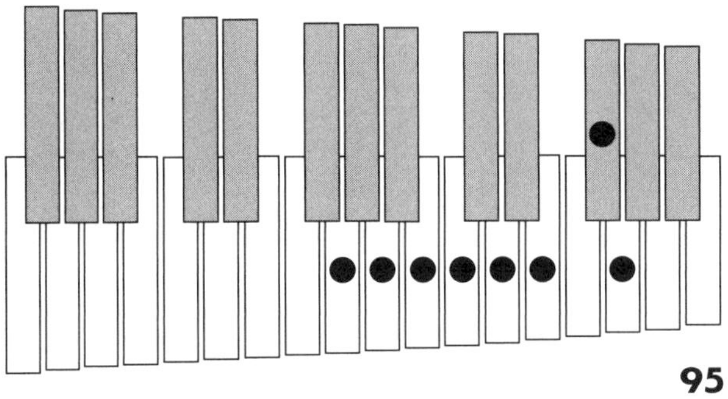

A Fresh Approach to Mallet Percussion
Accompaniment MP3 Track List

TRACK #	LINE #	SONG TITLE	INTRO COUNTS & MEASURES
1 / 2	8	Hot Cross Buns	8 counts (2 measures)
3 / 4	9	Au Claire de Lune	8 counts (2 measures)
5 / 6	13	Music Reading	8 counts (2 measures)
7 / 8	18	Lightly Row	8 counts (2 measures)
9 / 10	20	Baa, Baa, Black Sheep	8 counts (2 measures)
11 / 12	21	Jolly Old St. Nicholas	8 counts (4 measures in 2/4)
13 / 14	24	Skip to My Lou	8 counts (2 measures)
15 / 16	26	Oh, Susannah	7 counts (2 measures with the pickup)
17 / 18	27	Shortnin' Bread	8 counts (2 measures)
19 / 20	28	Rakes of Mallow	8 counts (2 measures)
21 / 22	30	Erie Canal	7 counts (2 measures with the pickup)
23 / 24	33	Old MacDonald	8 counts (2 measures)
25 / 26	35	When the Saints Go Marchin' In	13 counts in 4/4 (4 measures with the pickup)
27 / 28	37	American Patrol	15 counts in 4/4 (4 measures with the pickup)
29 / 30	38	Surprise Symphony	8 counts in 2/4 (4 measures)
31 / 32	42	Yankee Doodle	8 counts in 2/4 (4 measures)
33 / 34	43	Serenade	12 counts in 3/4 (4 measures)
35 / 36	46	All Men Are Brothers	8 counts in 4/4 (2 measures)
37 / 38	47	Simple Gifts	8 counts in 4/4 (2 measures)
39 / 40	50	Russian Sailor's Dance	8 counts in 2/4 (4 measures)
41 / 42	51	Turkey in the Straw	7 counts in 4/4 (2 measures with the pickup)
43 / 44	53	William Tell Overture	4 counts in 2/4 (2 measures)
45 / 46	55	Largo from Dvorak's Sym #9	4 counts in 4/4 (1 measure)
47 / 48	56	Hunter's Chorus	8 counts in 2/4 (4 measures with the pickup)
49 / 50	58	Orpheus in the Underworld	8 counts in 2/4 (4 measures)
51 / 52	59	Battle Hymn of the Republic	7 counts in 4/4 (2 measures with the pickup)
53 / 54	61	Soldier's March	4 counts in 2/4 (2 measures)
55 / 56	62	Irish Washerwoman	4 counts in 6/8 (2 measures with the pickup)
57 / 58	63	Jesu, Joy of Man's Desire	6 counts in 9/8 (2 measures)
59 / 60	64	The Sorcerer's Apprentice	6 counts in 9/8 (2 measures)
61 / 62	63	Clementi Sonatina	4 counts in cut time (2 measures)

* First track listed includes solo line, 2nd track listed is accompaniment WITHOUT solo.